THE ULTIMATE GUIDE TO NOVEL WRITING FOR BEGINNERS

Discover all the elements needed to write a fiction book from scratch. For writers who want to go from a blank page to a book their readers will love.

HACKNEY AND JONES

Also Published by Hackney and Jones

How to Write a Novel from Scratch

How to Write a Novel from Scratch is created BY authors FOR authors. It guides you from day one, helping you to come up with an exciting book idea from the very start. How to Write a Novel from Scratch covers the WHOLE process of writing a book through clear, logical steps. Simply fill in the blanks. AVAILABLE NOW

GRAB YOUR FREEBIE!

Creative Writing Prompts

Creative Writing Prompts will give you tonnes of deas to get your creative juices flowing. What story will you discover?

Ok, so how do I get my FREE book?

EASY! See the next page

GRAB YOUR FREEBIE!

Instructions:

1. Open the camera or the QR reader application on your smartphone.
2. Point your camera at the QR code to scan the QR code.
3. A notification will pop-up on screen.
4. Click on the notification to open the website link

Contents

Introduction — xi
Your Why — xxi
Foundations Of A Great Book — xxv

1. The Fiction Square — 1
2. Titles — 10
3. The Genre Bundle — 16
4. Crime Books - Do's and Don't's — 34
5. Endings — 40
6. How Many Characters Will I Need? — 49
7. Characters - Part 1 — 53
8. Characters - Part 2 — 57
9. Character Quirks — 61
10. Extended Character Descriptions — 65
11. Character Freestyle Points — 68
12. Character Arcs — 70
13. Research — 77
14. Locations — 86
15. Plot Twist Ideas: Make Your Readers Go WOW! — 91
16. The Wallop Scene - An Explanation — 97
17. The Wallop Scene — 101
18. The Basics — 104
19. The Basic Plan — 107
20. Your Opening Line — 111
21. The Almost Final Plan — 116
22. The Complete Plan For Writing Your Book — 124
23. Conclusion — 142

Advice On Writing By Fellow Authors	145
Angela Marsons - Crime Fiction	147
Emma Robinson – Writer of Women's Emotional Fiction	149
Donna Ashcroft – Feel Good Cosy Women's Fiction	151
Peter James – Crime Fiction	155
Cara Hunter – Psychological Thrillers	157
Books We Recommend	159
Also Published by Hackney and Jones	161
Feedback	163

Introduction

Welcome to **The Ultimate Guide to Novel Writing for Beginners.** This guide has been written specifically to accompany the **'How to Write a Novel from Scratch'** workbook and aims to offer the crib notes to help explain the point of including all the sections within this workbook when you plan and write all of your novels.

Why have we written this guide for you? Well, we were getting asked the same question over and over again; *"How'd you come up with ideas? How do you plan your plot twists? How do you come up with character names?"* So, this guide aims to answer the questions we get asked the most and to consolidate all the answers in one space. It might seem like the information contained within this guide is overwhelming in parts - because there are so many elements to writing a book - but each chapter in this guide not only aims to answer the questions we get asked, but also give you a strategy to implement the answer. Together, and with the **'How to Write a Novel from Scratch'** workbook by your side, we will literally build a book with you as we go along.

According to a survey, 81% of Americans feel they have a book in them. But what's interesting is actually how many people *do* get around to writing that book. In actual fact, it's less than 1%. When we found this out we couldn't believe how low that number was, and then we got to thinking why this might be.

What is stopping all these people from writing that book inside them?

Is it because it's such a big commitment, time-wise? Is it fear of starting? Fear of failing? Or even fear of succeeding? Are people scared that they might actually complete their book and are like, "now what?"

We then started to wonder if the reason was the fear of starting. We thought, 'what is it that people *need*, to realise their dream of writing a book?'

The answer was simple. They need a step-by-step guide, and a workbook to go alongside it, full of easy-to-fill-in writing templates, that will literally walk them through each basic element. They need a way of "building a book" from scratch - from the first word to the last. A no-fluff guide with easy-to-follow instructions. A strategy that never fails to deliver; one that can be rolled out every time you want to write a new novel.

And here it is. Held within the pages of this guide - and the accompanying **'How to Write a Novel from Scratch'** workbook - is all you will ever need to go from a blank page to a compelling first draft. We are so excited to bring this to you as we know in a very short space of time you are going to become a member of the 1% - the very elite group of those people who not only start writing a novel but actually complete it. You will be able to say to your friends and family, "Oh, I've written a book" or even, "I've written two or three books." You may even realise your dream of earning a living from your books. It's all possible.

As you can see from the image below, we've written quite a few books, including the fiction books below, and some non-fiction. We originally started out in the historical fiction genre with the Shona Jackson series, and now we've dipped our toe into crime fiction, which we're loving at the moment, with the **DI Rachel Morrison series.** This series is available to buy on Amazon now.

If you're anything like us, you'll get addicted to writing stories and books, because you've now got in your possession the strategy and successful formula from this time spent reading this guide.

This guide aims to give you the tools to create a well-written first draft that you can be *proud* of, using all the skills, secrets, strategies, techniques that we will teach you. You will learn what specific elements a book should contain to make it a gripping page-turner. Used together with our **'How to Write a Novel from Scratch'** workbook, nothing is stopping you from realising your dream.

We, ourselves, use the combination of this guide and the accompanying workbook every time we plan a new book. That's how we can be so sure it works. All you have to do is fill in the blanks in the workbook and a book appears before your eyes.

There's no getting around the fact that fiction readers have high expectations. There are a billion books out there they can choose to buy and read. Reader's tend to be exceptionally discerning in the crime genre particularly. When they download a crime book from whether it be Amazon or any other shop, or whatever, they are expecting a certain pattern. If you, as the author, don't know what that pattern is, you're going to find out in the reviews your readers leave you, believe me. This guide is going to show you exactly, step by step, what readers would expect, and how to leave out the guesswork.

The sections we will cover in this guide, which also mirror the sections in the workbook (with the addition of some bonus chapters in this guide) are as follows:

- **The Foundations of a Great Book** – This section of the guide covers what your readers expect from a great novel.
- **The Fiction Square: Workbook section 1** – This section covers how to initially come up with ideas for your novel. The reason for this section being at the beginning of the workbook is that whenever we've run polls on social media asking people what their biggest struggles with writing are, "coming up with ideas" is almost always right up there at the top.
- **Titles: Workbook section 2** – This section of the workbook deals with how to come up with a great title, so your readers will pick up your book over somebody else's. It's not by luck. It's not by fluke. There's a formula to this. In this chapter, we will show you a technique of how to come up with unique titles.
- **The Genre Toolkit: Workbook section 3** - Personally, this section is one of our favourite parts of the workbook, and something that we've spent a lot of time on. It is the complete blueprint to what is expected by readers from a crime book, and the conventions that all the bestsellers follow. So, no more guesswork and no more "I really hope my book does well." Once you know what's in the genre toolkit, you won't go back.
- **Crime Books – Do's and Don'ts: Workbook section 4** - This section of the workbook contains invaluable advice, gained from our experience so you don't make the same mistakes as we did early on.

- **Endings: Workbook section 5** – In this section of the workbook we look at how to make your endings really, really good, and what the impact is for different endings. We discuss when would you use a certain ending if you've got a series (or if you've got a standalone), and what your readers will be expecting in the next book.
- **Characters - How many characters will you need?: Workbook section 6** - In this extended workbook section on characters, we will look at what types of characters work best to drive the narrative? We get asked quite a lot, "can a story just be two characters? Can it be one character? Can it be four?" In this chapter, we'll give you the very basic formula as to how many characters to include to make your story compelling.
- **Characters Part 1: Workbook section 7**
- **Characters Part 2: Workbook section 8**
- **Character Quirks: Workbook section 9** - In this section of the workbook we will look at how you give your characters some quirks. These are specific individualities that will make the character more interesting to the reader.
- **Extended Character Descriptions: Workbook section 10** - In this section of the workbook we will further develop our character descriptions by giving them more features to add depth to their actions and motivations.
- **Character Freestyle Points: Workbook section 11** - In this section of the workbook we will look at freestyling ideas with your characters and imagining them in different situations, how they would act, what they wouldn't do, how they would be feeling etc… Once you start to experiment with your characters, you can start to imagine them in everyday situations. When you're writing the book in its entirety, you no longer have to think, "Well, what would my characters do in this situation?" A lot of this guide is about the prep work. It's almost like that saying, which is, "Train hard,

fight easy." When you come to the writing part, it's almost effortless.

- **Character Arcs: Workbook section 12** – In this section of the workbook we will discover why these are massively important in a story. The absence of a decent character arc was one of the things that we didn't give due diligence to when we first started writing. Now giving all characters an arc throughout the narrative is central to what we do when we're writing a book now. This section deals with the importance of character arcs, how to create them and who to do it for. Character arcs make your story even more believable, readable, compelling, and exciting.

- **Research: Workbook section 13** – This section of the workbook covers why doing the appropriate and adequate research is crucially important to your novel planning. If you ever look at a best-selling book, the one or two stars in reviews normally focus either on characters, or research, and the lack of it. The purpose of this workbook section is that we don't want you to make the same mistake as some authors make, which is to not put the effort into the research of each location or character. We show you all the different ways you can research for your book so your book does come alive and looks professional.

- **Locations: Workbook section 14** - This section of the workbook is to give you some ideas of locations as to where your novel can be set.

- **Plot Twist Ideas – Make Your Readers Go WOW!: Workbook section 15** - This is, without doubt, one of our favourite parts of a story. We love plot twists! We love watching them in a movie or a series, and we love writing them. In every single book of ours, there is normally an absolute whopper of a plot twist, and there's normally lots of little ones along the way. These are a lot of fun to plan and write, but monumentally disappointing to a reader if you do them wrong. This section of the workbook will help to inspire you with some awesome plot twists that will make your readers' jaws drop.

- **The Wallop Scene - An Explanation: Workbook section 16 -** This chapter includes a detailed explanation of what we mean by a "wallop scene".
- **The Wallop Scene: Workbook section 17** – This section of the workbook extends what we mean by the 'wallop scene'. This is a scene that makes you go, "Whoa, I wasn't expecting that. That's woken me up." We'll cover the importance of the wallop scene, where to put it and how to execute it successfully. Once you start including wallop scenes in your writing, your readers will appreciate it!
- **The Basics: Workbook section 18 -** This section of the workbook covers who your main character is, who is the ally, what is the main character's external goal, who is the antagonist, and what is the rough ending of the novel.
- **The Basic Plan: Workbook section 19 -** This section of the workbook goes through the basic three-act structure of the novel, giving you the stimulus questions to fill in your thoughts.
- **The Opening Line: Workbook section 20** – This section of the workbook covers why the opening line is crucial to the story. It sets the mood and the tone, and it makes it where your readers will essentially stand up and go, "Hang on a minute. This sounds interesting," which is what you want.
- **The Almost-Final Plan: Workbook section 21 -** This section of the workbook acts as final checks to make sure we have included every part of the planning stage.
- **The Complete Plan To Writing Your Book: Workbook section 22** – This section of the workbook is where your plan comes together in one place. When you reach this part in the workbook, three-quarters of the work on your novel planning is already done. This is

where your book is waiting for you to start writing the first page.

- **Advice from established bestselling authors** – This section of the guide is one we are very excited for you to read, and one we're very proud of. We reached out to some amazing authors who are bestsellers on Amazon, not just in their category, but bestsellers in the whole of Amazon, such as the amazing and prolific crime writer, Angela Marsons, who was so kind in just giving us the answers to some questions about her technique, her process, how she gets over her struggles. We interviewed several best-selling authors, to give you just even more value. So it's not even just our advice. You're getting the advice of people that are smashing it in their game.
- **Resources** – This section of the guide is a rundown of all resources that we've used personally, that we recommend to strengthen your game even more.

We will also cover along the way how to write effective, authentic-sounding dialogue. The importance of strong, believable dialogue is crucial in your writing as it is the voice of your characters. If the words they say aren't believable then the character won't be either. Dialogue can sometimes confuse a lot of people because they either write too much or not enough, or it's not believable, or this is where we call where people start 'info-dumping'. This section is designed to remove all the guesswork for you. You will learn how to set the appropriate pace of a scene just by using dialogue, and the difference between when men, women and children talk. The purpose of this section of the guide is to help you cut out clunky dialogue and make your characters sound more authentic.

By the end of this guide, you will be equipped with all of what you need to start writing without the fear of the dreaded writer's block. You will know what should go in each chapter to make sure that the novel you write will be classed as a 'page turner'. You will learn what drives your readers forward into the next chapter? Why should they read on? We're going to let you in on the secrets, what we do to make it so your readers just feel compelled to keep reading, and reading, and reading.

In general, it's a pretty detailed guide, as you can probably see. By the end of this guide, and when you have filled in the corresponding parts of the accompanying workbook, you will have created an amazing first draft that is in the perfect shape to be sent to your editor.

But before we start, let's take a moment to think about your 'why'. Why do you want to write a novel?

Your Why

Writing a book is one of the most personal journeys a person can go on. Every writer has their reasons for wanting to achieve this life goal, and each reason will be unique to them. Getting to the heart of that reason is the thing that you as a prospective writer will need to work out. Once you know *why* you are doing it, you will then be able to motivate yourself to start, and more importantly complete your first draft. No one can make you do it, and nor should they. What kind of book would be worth reading if it was forced out of an author's head begrudgingly? Writing a novel isn't compulsory. You do not have to do it. You should *want* to do it. And this is why your "why" is so important to discover. It will make those long days staring at your computer or writing pad worthwhile.

In the past, we've spoken to some writers, and they've said their "why" is simply because they wanted to write a book, just to see if they could. Some have even told us it was because then they can say when they're old and grey that they've written a book in their lifetime - which is an equally valid reason and should be celebrated too.

Quote by co-author, Vicky Jones:

'My "why" is simple. I started off writing one book for my Bucket List and then I quickly realised that it was super enjoyable, I found it extremely addictive. Then I thought, "hold on, I want to start making a living from this".'

So, is writing essentially a hobby, or is it a business? When you write for a hobby, you're writing what you want. You're not even worried about how it comes across, or how it sounds. You're not worried about sticking to a certain rule, and you'll just write as you go along. There might be a certain character that you've always wanted to explore and you just want to get that down on paper. Essentially, you're going through the process to say, 'I've written a book because it's on a bucket list', but then normally during the process, you start to enjoy it more.

Before you realise it, your hobby has opened your eyes to how enjoyable you found writing. Then the natural evolution of that thought process is that you start to think that others might enjoy what you write. Then you have to start playing by certain rules - conventions that readers expect in the genre that you write in. For example, if you're going to write a crime novel and it's all very "pink and fluffy", it's quite funny, the front cover is bright and colourful just because you like bright colours, then these factors do not fit the genre codes and conventions. More to the point, your front cover will stand out in all the wrong ways from the others in the genre. This will seriously affect your sales, as readers won't understand your reasoning and even worse get annoyed by your lack of research into what is appropriate in your genre of choice. And don't get us started on the reviews. Readers are not shy in telling you *exactly* what they thought of your novel, cover and all. Your debut novel might have been everything you wanted to write, but if you are serious about making a living out of your writing then, to speak plainly (this is a no-fluff guide after all) you must drop the ego and pay attention to the conventions that writers follow.

So, it's extremely important to think about your "why". If it's because you want to make a million pounds with your writing then it is entirely possible. There are a lot of traditionally published and self-published authors on Amazon that are making huge amounts of money with their books. But you need to treat your writing as a bone fide business, and marketing your books is key. Where traditional publishing is the thing that all writers strive for, partly because it gives your novel a certain kudos that a publishing house has taken a punt on you, and also, they cover the costs of publishing and marketing, it is by no means the only way to get your work out there. Self-publishing, using Amazon's game-changing platform Kindle Direct Publishing (KDP) is open to all. However, this method takes a lot of personal input and dedication - you are responsible not only for the writing of the manuscript but also for finding a decent editor, proofreader and cover designer, which unavoidably incurs costs. But like anything, the more effort and due diligence you put in then the more successful your product will be. The massive positive of self-publishing - and while we're on the subject, please forget the less-than-flattering term "vanity publishing" as it used to be called, as this is a grossly unfair way to regard what self-published authors are doing nowadays on Amazon - is that you keep much more of the royalty payment for each book sold. Traditionally published authors receive approximately 15% of each sale, self-published authors can make up to 70%. There are some self-published authors, such as Mark Dawson and Simon McCleave who are blazing a trail in their respective genres and making six and seven figures a year - and sometimes a month. The key to their success is marketing using ads.

Let's get that book out of your head first, shall we?

Foundations Of A Great Book

Let's begin our journey through the adventure of becoming an author by analysing the foundations of a great book. Not just any book, but a *great* book. To create a book that will wow your readers you will need to know what each book you write should contain to make it marketable to your readers and keep it true the genre that you're writing in. There are loads of codes and conventions that come with genre-specific writing, and it is your job to know and acknowledge these. Think of it in terms of when you buy a book or have watched a movie in the genre you love. Would you enjoy a gritty, hard-boiled crime book if it had a musical interlude and a load of dancing bears slap bang in the middle of it for absolutely no good reason? Or if you were reading a cosy romance and all of a sudden in chapter eight a knife-wielding maniac starts picking off each character one by one, would you be happy with this? Or would this generate a strongly-worded Amazon review? I'm guessing the latter.

The first major foundation of a good book is the compelling idea. This is the nugget of the story - its central plot. Next comes a great catchy title, or a title that makes the reader ask questions. This is crucial, as your book will be up against thousands, if not millions of other books, so you need to compel the reader to pick your book from the crowd.

Judging a book by its cover is an old cliché, but in this case, it is absolutely what happens. You choose a book usually because the cover art has piqued your interest. Next, you read the blurb (the back matter, which outlines the storyline and leaves you either wanting to continue your purchase or put it back on the shelf). Then, the next step in buyer behaviour is to look at the reviews on that book. We all do it, and we tend to look at the one-stars (if it has any) first. This is because we are programmed to look at what is wrong with a product more than why people liked it. We naturally want to know what "we are getting ourselves into" when we buy a product, and books are no different. And, we are naturally nosy species. We want to do a bit of digging around into other peoples' experiences with the thing we are about to buy. So, after you've read the reviews and filtered out all the unfair ones which moan about things beyond the author's control (this happens a lot so get used to it. Consumers do downgrade a product because of a poor delivery service or a bad condition it arrived in. However, most of the time you can email Amazon and ask them to remove this review as it doesn't reflect the quality of the product as such) you can then make your decision on whether you like the book enough to sneakily read the first few pages. You can do this on Amazon as it has a 'look inside' feature, which usually gives you around 10% of the book to preview. After reading this preview, you will know if you are "hooked in" enough to buy the book - and this is the same for your customers. They will now be expecting a great opening chapter, believable characters, awesome plot twists, red herrings, false heroes, wallop scenes and the usual three-act structure (beginning, middle and end).

The correct pace and build-up of tension throughout the narrative are also crucial foundations to a book, ones that must be done with a deft hand. If you drag your book on to get to a climax that is completed in two pages then this will annoy the reader. There should be a slow burn and gradual build-up to the wow moment where the killer's mask is metaphorically ripped off. You need to craft your book to provide a skilful and satisfying ending - preferably one the reader did not see coming. This of course does not include stories that are based on true stories, as anyone who knows the case will know how it ends, but in theory, you should still be able to take the reader on a satisfying journey throughout the narrative with skilful writing. They will still enjoy the ride, even if they already know the route.

So, throughout this guide, we are going to look at each of the areas that will help you create the foundations of a great book, and get you on the road to that novel that's stuck in your head. Each step will be manageable and have actionable solutions. Remember, this guide works perfectly hand in hand with the **'How to Write a Novel from Scratch'** workbook, in which you will find all the writing templates and sheets you'll need for planning. So if you haven't got this yet, order now from Amazon.

1

The Fiction Square

How to Write a Novel from Scratch - Workbook section 1

THIS CHAPTER IS all about how to come up with great ideas for a book. And this is the million-dollar question for prospective authors, as a lot of people like the *idea* of writing a book but they don't have any ideas they get excited about, or their ideas might be so niche that they wouldn't sell. We're going to show you a nifty way of getting your creative juices flowing by linking individual ideas. Once you learn the techniques we are going to show you, you can repeat them to create more books in the future.

THE FICTION SQUARE is a series of individual categories, writing prompts if you will, where you pick one from each category and link them together. It always reminds us of the numbers round in the TV quiz show Countdown. The old, "I'll have one from the top and the rest from anywhere else" decision of which number cards will go in the sequence on the board, which then generates a sum the contestants have to figure out how was calculated.

. . .

WE'RE a huge believer in using writing prompts when you are first starting out. They give you ideas you may never have thought of linking together, then when you link them you think, "actually, that works". Writing prompts always set us off down a path of creativity. When we were part of a writing group before we wrote our debut novel, **Meet Me At 10**, we had writing competitions a lot of time. These competitions started with just a writing prompt, whether that was one word, a single sentence, or an image. With these writing prompts it is also important not to edit your thought at this stage. We know this is very difficult to do, as we naturally want to tweak and shape our initial singular thought. But wait until you have connected your category thoughts, as then you will have a complete picture of all the elements you'll need.

LET's now take a look at **The Fiction Square** section in our **'How to Write a Novel from Scratch'** workbook. Here you will see you have columns headed:

Character Occupation
Object
Setting/Location
Motivation
Obstacle

USE THIS FICTION SQUARE TO CREATE ENDLESS IDEAS! PICK ONE THING FROM EACH COLUMN AND USE THESE AS YOUR INSPIRATION

CHARACTER OCCUPATION	OBJECT	SETTING/ LOCATION	MOTIVATION	OBSTACLE
SOLDIER	KEY	BEACH	JUSTICE	RUNNING OUT OF TIME
PRINCESS	CAR	CHURCH	GREED	HEALTH
TEACHER	LETTER	SCHOOL	LOVE	SECRET GETS EXPOSED
DOCTOR	A CLOCK	ANOTHER PLANET	SUCCESS	INJURED

IN THE EXAMPLE BELOW, we have chosen the following:

CHARACTER OCCUPATION: **Soldier**
    Object: **Letter**
    Setting/Location: **Beach**
    Motivation: **Love**
    Obstacle: **Time running out**

THE IDEA this has given us for our story is:

The main character is a man who gets handed a letter from a dying soldier on Normandy beach during World War 2. Time is running out and the man needs to deliver this love letter before the soldier's sweetheart back home is due to get married to somebody else.

THIS IS ONLY A VERY rough first idea, and the flaws are there for all to see (if the soldier is dying then why would his sweetheart getting married again be a worry?) but this gives us some substance to work with. Maybe the soldier's only motivation to keep living is the idea that his mortal enemy back home won't be able to marry his sweetheart, but she is convinced the soldier is already dead so wavering towards this enemy and his proposal should the soldier not return from the war. So, we could tweak this initial idea to the soldier is fighting the odds, given his injuries, on the promise that his letter reaches his sweetheart in time, with news he is still alive so she holds off a bit longer from getting with this new man. This now gives us an urgency for our main character to get the letter dispatched as soon as possible. After a little more ironing out, this idea could have some legs. But if you go off this idea, you can still use the parts of it that work, or simply return to **The Fiction Square** and start over. Either way, you have succeeded in getting your juices flowing.

LET'S use the example fiction square in our workbook again. This time we are going to choose:

CHARACTER OCCUPATION: **Doctor**
    Object: **Car**
    Setting/Location: **School**
    Motivation: **Justice**
    Obstacle: **Health**

THIS HAS GIVEN us an idea straight away. What if:

A doctor, who has recently lost a teenage patient on the operating table, finds out that the janitor of the local school is the one who caused the car crash which put his patient in the hospital. In the absence of proof, as there was no CCTV and no evidence that the crash was anything but an accident, the doctor plans to exact revenge on the janitor when he discovers the janitor has a hidden reason for trying to kill the teenager.

AGAIN, you can see that in just a few minutes this idea has formed, brewed and generated a great idea to possibly pursue. With **The Fiction Square**, the ideas are endless. All you need is the five ideas - one from each category column - and you begin to ask the key questions with each prompt; who, what, why, when and how. In this second idea, who is the doctor/janitor, what have they done, why have they done it, when did they do it and how. Freestyle it until your idea becomes all you can think about. Then start jotting down ideas and sub-plots. You may even start to add more characters and locations.

CAN you see how addictive it becomes?

NOW WE CAN START to widen out further with our basic 5-part idea:

- When is the action taking place?
- Where is our first scene taking place?
- Do we see the crash?
- Do we start with the crash team trying to save the teenager on the operating table?
- Do we start the story as the crash happens?

JUST BY WRITING these questions down from this prompt, you start to completely open up your mind but do not edit at this stage. Also, you will naturally start to drift into a genre you enjoy reading. This is fine and actively encouraged as this will sustain your attention span. However, throughout this guide, and the accompanying workbook, we will delve into other genres and the ins and outs of each, so you never know, you may decide to deviate from your more familiar science fiction and dabble in a bit of cosy romance for the first time. Never rule anything out.

WRITING prompts can also come from stories from local newspapers. You'd be surprised to learn how many authors do this. they read the news, find an intriguing story then use it as the nucleus for their next bestseller. One of our favourite authors, and someone we've been honoured to have communicated with during our writing career, is Peter James. He is a very successful crime writer and has recently had an ITV drama made from his **Roy Grace**

series. He uses this newspaper method when coming up with new ideas for his plot lines and characters. He doesn't use actual people from the articles he reads and blurs the lines of the stories just enough for them not to be identified, but it works well for him and gives him the basis of characters that are authentic and human. Sometimes, as Peter James has found, the intriguing stories are in local news. So just literally Google the news in your local area to generate some juicy ideas. Or even try further afield - if you live in a city, look at surrounding suburban areas - as you will see how different characters can react in different environments. A smorgasbord of ideas is just waiting between the sheets of a newspaper for you to discover.

EXAMPLES OF LOCAL NEWS:

A TRADITIONAL village pub will remain closed for the rest of the week following a fire last weekend.

HMMM... was it arson? Was it an accident? Were the perpetrators hoping to get rid of evidence? Were they caught in the act? If so, what will they do next?

Glasgow road blocked off after flytipper dumps huge pile of rubbish overnight

IN THE NEWS

DURING THE CLEAN-UP OPERATION, was something discovered? Were the perpetrators caught dumping the rubbish and fled the scene?

Teenager arrested after man found dead in street

WHO WAS THE MAN? Who was the teenager? Was it mistaken identity? If so, who was the intended target?

Was it a mugging gone wrong?

> NEWS
>
> **US soldier loses 1 Afghan translator; fights to save another**

WE CAN IMAGINE this being a Military Fiction story, can you?

YOU GET the picture because news is happening ALL THE TIME, you will NEVER EVER run out of inspiration. Thank you, Peter James, for that tip!

ALTERNATIVELY, if fiction squares don't work for you, you could simply brainstorm your ideas as they come into your head. Free write what would happen if:

- A dog could talk.
- A five-year-old could predict the future.
- A salt-of-the-earth policeman turns spy for the enemy.
- A house cleaner turns out to be a serial killer/assassin.

AS WE'VE PREVIOUSLY SAID, DO NOT EDIT at this stage. There's no right or wrong at this point in the planning, and no one marking your work. You can pretty much get away with anything right now.

. . .

LET's take the first idea - the talking dog. How do you sustain this idea past it being a gimmick? Well, now we need complications to the narrative. What if the dog loses his voice right at the crucial moment in the story? How does the dog overcome this? Does he have a helper? What is riding on his ability to get his voice back in time? What are the stakes?

Now, we can start to have some fun and add some combinations together. You could pick two of the above options at random to make your story more interesting. What if the dog that can talk met a five-year-old who can predict the future? Or what if the reason the five-year-old can predict the future is that she's the only one who can hear the dog talk and it's the dog who can predict the future? Therefore, if the dog can no longer talk then the girl can no longer predict the future, so the storyline develops with more drama in this way. And now someone is in danger because of this. The stakes have been raised and the narrative ramps up in tension. A simple idea, but one that can be developed a great deal.

ANOTHER IDEA COULD BE a murderer who wants to solve cold cases gets involved somehow with a policeman-turned-spy - a role reversal in some respects. What if the policeman uncovered that the murderer was innocent and trying to solve the case that put him in prison? Does the policeman help him prove his innocence, even though it was the very same policeman who put him there in the first place? As you start to flesh out your ideas, you can then begin to think about the "how, who, what, when, where and why" in the story. What is the overall theme? Maybe police corruption? Before you know it, your idea will have begun to take shape and got you super excited to start writing.

So, to sum up, **The Fiction Square** is a brilliantly simple way of getting your creative juices flowing, giving you key elements as basic ideas. With a little bit of free writing, these ideas become a storyline you can get your teeth into writing. Now, we move on to thinking up a title for your book - one that will hook your readers instantly.

2

Titles

How to Write a Novel from Scratch - Workbook section 2

So, you've got your ideas all sketched out on your writing pad and you're all ready to get cracking. Now we're going to turn our attention to the second chapter in our **'How to Write a Novel from Scratch'** workbook - **Titles.** This is where you are going to start thinking about a title for your story. It can't just be any old title though. It needs to, as we writers say, "pop". This means it needs to encourage the reader to ask questions in their head about the book. You want your title to separate you from the millions of other titles out there. You want people to choose your book because something about the title intrigues them enough that they cannot help themselves from wondering what the title means or refers to. In this chapter, we will explain how this is done.

MUCH OF THE advice that follows is very dependent on you understanding your genre. For example, if you write books for children, especially young children, you will probably find that your titles are very literal and straightforward - **'Spot the Dog'** is a book about a dog called Spot, for example. The **Harry Potter series** of books by J.K. Rowling is aimed at older children, and is titled using the object/place/villain that Harry Potter is facing within the story, so again, quite 'cut-to-the-chase' straightforward. This is because kids have no time for abstract titles. they want to know what the story is about straight from the title - they're very busy creatures, you know!

IF YOU ARE WRITING for the adult market, you can start to think about more abstract titles. This is especially common in literary fiction. **'The Light Between Oceans'** draws you in straight away and encourages you to ask questions - which oceans? What is the 'light' they speak of? **'Where The Crawdads Sing'** is another example. What are crawdads and why is it significant where they sing? These are questions that immediately spring to mind. There are thousands more, but you get the idea.

ABOVE ALL, don't just simply settle for a title for your horror or crime book like, 'The Murderer', as this is very boring. The reader will be thinking, "ok, so there is a murderer. Great. I kinda expected that given the genre of book it is" and roll their eyes before swiftly moving on from your book to the next more intriguing one. Your title must be abstract enough to make the reader ask questions, but not too abstract that they have no sense whatsoever about the relevance of the title to your plot line. Your title is extremely important to get in the bag before you start writing, especially if your title is the key plot twist or guides you through the narrative yourself as you write.

WITH CRIME FICTION, you do want to make your title sound a bit more intriguing. Let's take the bare bones of an idea we had earlier - our wrongly convicted criminal wants to reopen the case he was convicted for to prove his innocence, and whilst doing so he uncovers loads of unsolved cold cases. Now, the title, 'Cold Case' is pretty mundane and boring, so what can we do to juice it up? You could start to brainstorm word associations for the word 'cold'. The words, 'ice', 'blue' and 'stone' spring to mind, but also, we're starting to think of bodies and bones. After all, a cold case is defined as such by the length of time it has remained unsolved. So, a body involved would now be just bones potentially. Now we have in our minds the words 'cold' and 'bones'. Don't edit at this point. Just keep writing words down that speak to you. Remember, you have sketched out the initial blueprint for your story, so you will have a good idea of how you want it to go.

Now, instead of the title, 'Cold Case', our brain is thinking, 'Cold Bones'. Much more intriguing, as this gives the reader a sense that there may be an indication of a burial place within the story, such as the cold water or a snowdrift, for example. Let's develop our title more. Maybe the bones lead the innocent man to more clues about his case? Almost as if the bones are telling a story through the clues they have left. Now we're thinking of the title, 'The Talking Bones' and 'The Bones That Speak'. A long way from refined and perfect (and still a little on the cliché side) but it's much more effective than our first idea, 'Cold Case'.

START TO THINK about the visions your title gives you also. Write down every word that you can think of that relates to the central idea of 'cold' and 'bones' then start to circle the words you like the sound of. The general rule of thumb is that if *you* find it intriguing then your reader should also.

NEXT, once you have your central idea, start to think about a location where you would like to set your action. We were speaking to a writer friend of ours recently as we were helping her to develop her story. She wanted to set her novel in Amsterdam during wartime. We said to her, "write down all the things that Amsterdam is known for, such as its beauty, culture, its architecture and above all its colour - namely from its tulip fields. Then start joining up these ideas." We then typed 'Amsterdam' into Google and saw golden statues, and then put them together in our minds with the tulips and ideas began to flow in our heads. We passed these on to our friend and together we came up with titles such as 'The Golden Tulip', which tied in nicely with her storyline, as it included a sunset scene. Already, we could picture the front cover of the book with a very similar image in mind - a woman waiting for her lover to come home from the war, looking far off into the sunset as the day he was supposed to come home has passed. Very evocative, and fits perfectly with the title, with a tulip field in the background behind her.

ANOTHER TOP TIP is to think about the *opposite* to the themes and locations you have written down in your brainstorm. For example, if your crime or horror fiction book is set in the Caribbean, which has a traditionally warm climate, you could think of what is the opposite to warm to create a sinister feeling - an otherness to what the reader expects, which could mirror the novel's protagonist/antagonist. So, your title could be, 'The Cold Caribbean', which works alliteratively too.

WHEN YOU LOOK on Amazon at the titles of the books in your genre, you will notice that there are similarities in terms of how many words the authors use in their titles. For example, for psychological dramas, the authors tend to use few words, and each word packs a punch - such as, 'The Stepmother', 'Trust No-one', Her Final Words', I Found You', 'Three Perfect Liars', and 'See Them Run'. With Romance novels you tend to see longer titles, such as, 'An Unusual Bride for the Unloved Duke', The Giver of Stars', 'It Started with a Secret' and 'The Mail-Order Bride's Stolen Groom'.

TAKE a look in your **'How to Write a Novel from Scratch'** workbook at the section which asks you to sum up the book. Do so. Write down the central idea of your book and then circle all the words that intrigue you. These words will give you something to work from for an intriguing title.

THE NEXT SECTION in the workbook will prompt you to look on Amazon at the other titles in your chosen genre. What kinds of words do these books use in their titles? Do they focus on an object? A theme? A specific name? Or even a place? Think of your novel idea now. Your ideas for your title should be racing through your head by now. What questions do you think your readers will ask of your novel just from the title? Don't forget to use the blank space in your workbook to jot down your ideas so you don't forget them.

YOU WILL SEE from the workbook, at the end of the **Titles** chapter, that there are three spaces for you to jot down your three favourite titles and what questions you think the readers will ask. The purpose of this is to enable you to pick the best, most effective title. Make sure you use this space as it is designed for you to whittle down the best, most marketable option from your bank of ideas.

ANOTHER TIP IS for you to run a poll to your audience (if you have one) or simply ask 10-20 people you know, especially if they love reading to pick the best title.

REMEMBER, it is about attracting readers, not what your favourite is.

IF YOU ADHERE to what is selling in your genre and you follow that model - remember you're not "copying" you are emulating - then readers in your genre will class you as a bone fide member of the genre club and potentially give your book a shot, as it fits within their requirements. On this score, it is better to fit in than stand out.

. . .

THE QUALITY of your story and writing is what will make you stand out.

NEXT, we are going to look at the next chapter in our **'How to Write a Novel from Scratch'** workbook, and laser-focus on a particular genre and all its parts, so that when you write a novel in this genre you are remembering everything you should be considering to make your novel the best version of itself. For this chapter, we have chosen to focus on the **crime genre**, as this is the genre we write in and feel we can offer you lots of value and benefit from our experiences. Let's dive straight in.

3

The Genre Bundle

How to Write a Novel from Scratch - Workbook section 3

IN THIS CHAPTER, we will show you how you can incorporate all the elements of a genre into your writing and ensure that no stone is left unturned. For this chapter we are going to use a genre we are currently writing our fiction novels in, so you will receive the benefit of all the things we have learned - and all the mistakes we have learned from - so far.

BY USING the information contained within this **Genre Bundle** you will be taking the steps that your competition isn't and, in turn, elevate your chance of success. If you don't take heed of the information in this genre bundle you are likely to miss a vital ingredient and likely to miss the mark of what is expected by your readers - and they are not likely to give you another chance if your first book is rubbish with there being so many other choices out there on the market.

. . .

IN YOUR **'How to Write a Novel from Scratch'** workbook, this is the next section. Now, we've started with crime for the reason also that it's a very popular genre. This same genre bundle, however, can also apply to mystery, psychological, and also horror novels, as there are many elements to these genres that cross over quite a lot.

HOW WE CREATED **The Genre Bundle** was quite simple.

We looked at the top 50 books on Amazon in the crime genre and began to take notes of all the common elements within the blurbs and book descriptions. We also looked at the front covers, titles and keywords. Anyone who knows us knows we're lovers of data, so we began to spot patterns from the notes we'd made and worked out how to replicate these patterns to help fellow authors include all the elements which readers in these genres expect. The intention was to make sure no element was left out and to give authors the best possible chance of competing on a level playing field with established authors in these genres.

THE REST IS DOWN to the author, with the strength of their writing and individual novel plots and storylines. But fundamentally, the idea was that new authors' books would fit in seamlessly with other books in their genre using the advice in the genre bundle.

TO START WITH, we looked at **words** most frequently used in the blurbs of the top 50 books in the crime genre, as this is a massive part of what sells the book to the reader. We copied and pasted all the words and put them into a 'word cloud'. This is a tool easily downloadable from the internet and can help you see what the most common words used in a passage of writing are. With this list (that you will see in the workbook), authors can write their blurbs using the power words that appear most frequently in already-published and popular (as they are in the top 50) books, and give potential readers *exactly* what they are looking for.

Readers who like certain genres tend to hoover up everything similar to their favourite author, so they will find your novel too if it sounds as if it is in the same vein. The storyline will be different but the look, feel and sound of the novel will fit the reader's requirements. Remember, authors tend to release a couple of books a year, but readers read much more than that, so they will need options. Think about the 'also bought' category on Amazon - how do you think authors get their books in this row? Because readers have bought these books as well as their first choice when they logged on. How did they find these books to buy? Because they "sounded like their favourite book."

SIMPLE BUYER PSYCHOLOGY REALLY, when you think about it. You just have to put your book in their sights and in this instance, it is much better to fit in with the crowd than stand out. Especially if your book is available on Kindle, where readers don't have to think about clutter and space when buying books. We have an e-reader with hundreds of books on it and remember buying everything in the niche we were interested in at the time - so a lot of authors who followed the conventions of the genre, as found in the genre bundle here, did very well out of our shopping spree!

. . .

In your **'How to Write a Novel from Scratch'** workbook you will see the list of the most common words we found in our word cloud:

detective, case, discover, girl, home, murder, body, dead, dark, woman, house, young, years, behind, disappeared, friend, fear, found, help, happened, husband, wife, investigation, missing, killer, secrets, police, perfect, victim, watching, truth, reveals, past, man, knows, family, city, keep, kill, evidence, vanished.

By using this word cloud, your blurb will sound just as compelling as the bestsellers in your genre. Many of the words will no doubt appear in your novel idea, but it's very helpful to see what are the most common words used to ensure you are thinking along the right lines and on the right track to your first/next bestseller.

This word cloud can also set you on the road to new ideas for your novel. You can use the words to plug any gaps you have in your storyline, for example, have you missed the vital element in your crime/mystery/psychological/horror novel of your characters having 'secrets'?

The next step was to take some of these 'power words' from our word cloud and brainstorm some ideas for our novel. In the example in the **'How to Write a Novel from Scratch'** workbook, we chose the words:

girl, friend, police, perfect, watching, family, murder

THESE ARE the words that stood out to us, and already a nugget of an idea has formed just from looking at these words.

> *A young girl is reported missing by her best friend. The police investigate what looks like now to be a murder. The best friend comes from a perfect family. And when DCI Thomas* starts watching the family more closely, not everything is as it seems.*

*THIS NAME just popped into our head as we were thinking up this idea - see how easy it can come to you?

We made this idea up on the spot. It didn't even take two seconds. We just picked out five words from the most common words and came up with an idea. You might pick out 10 words, you might pick out three words. The main thing is that you don't edit anything at this stage. Let your ideas flow.

WHAT DO we call our characters?

Next, we come to thinking up **names** for our characters. But what is in a name? Why do authors pick certain names for their characters? Sometimes it's because they like that name, or have always wanted a 'Sam' or a 'James' to feature in a book they write, for their reasons. But not all names work in certain genres. You'll rarely have a leading hero called Barney or Timmy unless he's an unassuming hero who steps in to save the day reluctantly - or a dog. Unfortunately, though, Barney or Timmy just aren't as enigmatic sounding as Max, Alex or Bruce are. It is a fact that stereotypes play a large part in the planning of novels especially with character names fitting their roles, whether it is conventions of these stereotypes, or breaking these conventions for the purposed of taking an alternative path with a subversive narrative.

. . .

A LOT of the content we've put together for the genre bundle is there because of feedback we've received when researching this and the **'How to Write a Novel from Scratch'** workbook. Lots of authors have told us that they struggle to come up with character names that are suitable for the professions the characters do and the genre of the story they appear in. As previously stated, it is an unavoidable fact that to use genre conventions in your writing you must adhere to a certain degree of stereotyping - readers identify with well-educated people being doctors or poorly educated people being petty thieves. Whether you like it or not, we all stereotype in our fiction, whether we are a reader or a writer. It's how we identify and love/loath characters when we picture them and tap into our preconceived ideas of them.

```
CHARACTER NAMES AND ROLES

HUSBAND, WIFE, YOUNG GIRL, LUCY, ELIZA, KERRY, EX-HUSBAND, PENNY, CATHERINE,
GEORGE, ALISON, RUTH, ADAM, JOSH, LILY, ALICE, ALICIA, JULES, WILL, IN-LAWS, GEMMA,
ELLIOT, CHLOE, PARENTS/A STRANGER, SUZI, MARY, ELLE, KIDNAPPER, FOUND GIRLS, HOLLY,
ELLA, MACK, SARAH, PARENTS, TWINS, OFFICER, HOMELESS MAN/WOMAN, NEIGHBOURS,
DAUGHTER, SAMMY, EDIE, BEN, SOPHIE, EMMA, NINA, MAGGIE, ALISON, A COLLEAGUE, A
FRIEND, ROY, LAURA, MEG, AN ELDERLY WOMAN, JAMIE, KIDNAPS FAMILY MEMBERS, A
SOMEBODY, TIM, TAMARA, POET, A DOCTOR, A TENANT, SKYE, DAVID, JOY, LILIAN, ZOE,
RUTH BOYLE, NICK, A BETRAYED WIFE/HUSBAND, SAMANTHA, FRANCES, A PATIENT, CONNIE,
LEWIS, STELLA, AN ALCOHOLIC, A CORONER, THE COMMUNITY, TRUDY, CLAIRE, BILLIE, KATE,
RESEARCH ASSISTANT, POLICE DETECTIVE, SARA, GAIL, A PATH, MAY, JANIE, A CHILD,
CHILDRENS SERVICES, CONSTRUCTION WORKERS, JACK, GANG LEADERS.

HOW CAN I USE THIS? LOTS OF PEOPLE HAVE TOLD ME THEY STRUGGLE TO
COME UP WITH CHARACTER NAMES SUITABLE FOR THAT GENRE. THE NAMES
AND JOB ROLES ARE THOSE THAT APPEAR WITHIN THE TOP 50 IN THE GENRE.

WHAT DO WE HAVE NOW?

A YOUNG GIRL IS REPORTED MISSING BY HER BEST FRIEND.

THE POLICE INVESTIGATE WHAT LOOKS TO NOW BE A MURDER.

THE BEST FRIEND COMES FROM A PERFECT FAMILY AND WHEN DCI THOMAS STARTS
WATCHING THE FAMILY MORE CLOSELY, NOT EVERYTHING IS AS IT SEEMS.

MY CHARACTERS ARE CALLED:
SOPHIE, THE YOUNG GIRL MISSING, 12 YEARS OLD
ALICE, THE BEST FRIEND, 14 YEARS OLD
MEG, THE MOTHER OF THE BEST FRIEND, HAS A DRINK PROBLEM
BEN, THE FATHER OF THE BEST FRIEND IS A CONSTRUCTION WORKER
DCI TOM NICHOLS, DETECTIVE LOOKING INTO IT
```

After seeking out the most common power words from the top 50 books in our genre (crime), we then looked at the most common character names and roles that appear in these books. You can see the full list in the **'How to Write a Novel from Scratch'** workbook in the genre bundle section. We then chose names and roles to fit our example from above, as follows:

LET's go back and revisit our example storyline from earlier:

A young girl is reported missing by her best friend. The police investigate what looks like now to be a murder. The best friend comes from a perfect family. And when DCI Thomas* starts watching the family more closely, not everything is as it seems.

WE'VE PICKED a couple of names from the list in the workbook that are found in crime novels that we feel would suit our characters.

OUR NAMES for our characters (using the list):

<u>Sophie</u>: a young girl who has gone missing. 12 yrs old.
Alice: best friend. 13 yrs old.
Meg: mother of the best friend. Has a drinking problem.
<u>Ben</u>: father of the best friend. Construction worker.
<u>DCI Tom Nichols</u>*: *the detective investigating the case.*

*We had second thoughts about the detective's name so changed it to DCI Tom Nichols - always feel free to tweak as you have new ideas as this is a perfectly natural evolution process to your planning.

So, you can see how the idea is starting to take shape?

NEXT, we started to think about the **events** that are taking place during the story.

WHERE COULD the action be taking place? A dinner party? A wedding? A funeral? For our example, we chose the event to be the funeral of the young girl, Sophie, who had gone missing.

. . .

HERE, DCI Tom Nichols observes the families in attendance and notices that the mother of Sophie's best friend Alice is acting suspiciously (we don't know what part she plays yet, remember, you don't need all the answers, you are just building at this stage).

OUR CHOICE of the event here clearly moves the action forward to there being an outcome to the disappearance, and it creates a sense of purpose for the investigating officer and moves the narrative forward giving your novel its edge. This can also act as what's known as the 'inciting incident' - something that kicks the story off and gets the narrative flowing.

YOU WILL ALSO NEED to have an idea when planning your story of the central **location** to the narrative, i.e where the main part of the action is set.

WAS somebody murdered at a wedding reception? Did someone disappear from a shopping centre? Did something terrible happen in a haunted house a hundred years ago? The list is endless, but we have compiled some common examples in your **'How to Write a Novel from Scratch'** workbook as inspirational ideas for you to choose from. Again, these have also been taken from the top 50 books in the crime genre - we've researched so you don't have to (please don't spend hours on research, get the damn workbook and save your sanity).

OUR EXAMPLE IS BUILDING NICELY NOW. Below we have included the event and location we have chosen to almost complete our novel idea.

A young girl, Sophie, is reported missing by her best

friend, Alice. The police investigate what looks like now to be a murder. Alice comes from a perfect family, her mother Meg and her construction worker father, Ben. Sophie's family live on the outskirts of town in an isolated cottage. But when DCI Tom Nichols starts watching Alice's family more closely at Sophie's funeral, not everything is as it seems, when he notices Alice's mother behaving suspiciously.

WE CHOSE 'FUNERAL' for my event as it made the most dramatic sense. We thought, "Well, we've already had someone murdered. So it makes sense that it's going to be her funeral." Also, with the mother of the best friend acting suspiciously it gets the reader thinking, 'why? Has she got anything to do with the murder? Is she having an affair with somebody who's at the funeral? Is she planning something herself? Is she planning to leave her husband?' It could be absolutely anything and now the fun starts as the story outline begins to build and expand.

FOR THIS IDEA, we haven't used anything other than the workbook and we love this book idea already!

THE LOCATION we chose from the list taken from the top 50 books in the crime genre was an isolated cottage on the outskirts of town. We felt this gave us an interesting hook, with the two young girls seemingly living on opposite ends of the town - Sophie, the young girl who has been murdered, and her family living on the outskirts away from society. Why? And how did they become friends living so far apart? Was it at school? Did Sophie wander into town? Did Alice, her best friend, wander *out* of town, away from her perfect family home?

THERE IS A DIVIDE HERE, which makes the story interesting, and stimulates the reader to want to investigate further by reading on.

WE NOW HAVE to start thinking of a suitable title for our novel. Again, so you don't have to, we have made a list of the titles of the top 50 books in the crime genre and cross-referenced the words used to give us a sense of the common themes. A full list can be found in the 'titles' section of your **'How to Write a Novel from Scratch'** workbook. From the 50 titles, you can see a pattern emerging. Here are a few examples:

Her Final Words
Trust No One
The Late Show
The Silent Patient
The Perfect Life
Here To Stay
Left For Dead

LOTS OF TITLES, especially in the crime genre, are quite sparse with words. They are short and punchy - **three words** seems to be very common, as seen by the list above we took from the top 50 books as listed on Amazon.

THREE WORDS GIVE the right balance between information and intrigue - and like any trend you see in books, it is always better to blend in than stand out, so it's highly advised to stick to this three-word title idea. Of course, there are always exceptions to every rule, and you will see books with four or even five words, but these extra words might include 'the' or 'a' or 'to' so judge for yourself if you count these. As long as you remember that less is more with regards to titles in the crime genre then you are fine and will fit in nicely with the other books in your genre.

. . .

LET'S REVISIT OUR EXAMPLE, and slot in a title idea or two. We used only words from the Power Words found in the workbook.

<u>Title:</u> *The Best Friend/The Talking Walls/The Silent Voice/The Cottage Lie/Secrets Within Walls*

A young girl, Sophie, is reported missing by her best friend, Alice. The police investigate what looks like now to be a murder. Alice comes from a perfect family, her mother Meg and her construction worker father, Ben. Sophie's family live on the outskirts of town in an isolated cottage. But when DCI Tom Nichols starts watching Alice's family more closely at Sophie's funeral, not everything is as it seems, when he notices Alice's mother behaving suspiciously.

OUR PERSONAL FAVOURITE? It has to be 'The Talking Walls'. It asks questions 'What are the walls 'saying'? Is it bad? Is it a warning?'

OUR NEXT CONSIDERATION is how to juice up our novel idea and turn it into a kind of blurb for the back matter of the book. We can do this by slotting in some **power words** into our idea. These are so-called because they pack a punch and strengthen the impact of your writing.

THERE IS A LONG, detailed list of power words that we have found in all the blurbs from the top 50 books in the crime genre on Amazon, and you can feel the punch from all of them. Words like 'shocking', 'nightmare', 'gripping', 'senseless', 'broken', 'deadly' and 'reckless' really do add depth and power to your sentences. They ignite a reader's interest and keep their hands on your book for that little bit longer.

THE LIST of power words in your **'How to Write a Novel from Scratch'** workbook can also be used if you are writing a book in the psychological, thriller or even horror genre - as can all of the genre bundle as a whole - it is quite a useful tool to help get your creative juices flowing so use each part as you see fit.

BY USING power words in your book description or blurb, you are setting the mood and atmosphere for your readers, and getting them to speculate what is happening. This is the first step to getting them to buy your book - which is the aim, right?

So, what power words have we chosen? Well, let's revisit our example one last time and slot in the power words that sprang from our long list (in the workbook).

Title: The Talking Walls

A young girl, Sophie, is reported <u>missing</u> by her best friend, Alice. The police investigate what looks like now to be a <u>disturbing</u> and <u>chilling</u> murder. Alice comes from a perfect family, her mother Meg and her construction worker father, Ben. Sophie's family live on the outskirts of town in an isolated cottage. But when DCI Tom Nichols starts watching Alice's family more closely at Sophie's funeral, not everything is as it seems, when he notices Alice's mother behaving suspiciously. And her pointed <u>silence</u> on the murder, and her daughter's relationship with the <u>victim</u>, only serves to lead Nichols to <u>suspect</u> them more - and adds to the <u>sinister</u> mystery of how Sophie came to die that day.

Power words used: disturbing, chilling, secrets, silence, sinister, missing, suspect, mystery, victim.

WE'RE HOOKED ALREADY!

AND THIS WAS CREATED in minutes!

AND THERE WE HAVE IT. We went from a very rough outline of the story at the start of the genre bundle, and now we have a very detailed, punchy and intriguing blurb outline for our novel. By using this genre bundle you are building a book, making sure you incorporate all the elements your readers will expect and which will make your central idea stand out.

WE NOW HAVE AN IDEA, character names and roles that fit the genre, the main event, a central location, a title and the power words to strengthen your descriptions.

IF YOU STICK to this formula, you are giving yourself every chance of your novel becoming a bestseller, just like the books we have been drawing our inspiration from. Top 50 here we come!

THE NEXT CONSIDERATION is how long should a book be in the crime/thriller/psychological genre be?

The consensus on this seems to be around the 55,000-65,000 word mark, as it's long enough for a decent story to be told, but short enough for it to keep the reader engaged and pack a punch. To new authors, 65,000 words sound a lot, but you simply break this down into manageable chunks, so you have a target word count to aim for in each writing session. As you can see from your **'How to Write a Novel from Scratch'** workbook the 65,000 words can be broken down into 2,000-words per day chunks, which is a very achievable amount to aim for.

IF YOU WRITE four times a week, at 2,031 words per day you will write 8,125 words per week. This means you will complete your first draft in 8 weeks. Exciting!

THIS SCHEDULE ISN'T TOO arduous and can fit around most work and home situations. Just think, in eight short weeks of focused work, you will have achieved a life goal!

AS WITH ANY type of activity, there are always things you should do and things you shouldn't do. Writing is no exception. There is a long, detailed list of these things in the **'How to Write a Novel from Scratch'** workbook so check them out.

ENSURE your novel planning includes the good things to do and avoids the things not to do. One of the worst things you can do is to forget to have a decent plot twist. Readers LOVE a good plot twist, some only read certain books in the hope of finding one. How many times have you read a thriller or crime book and thought you knew who the villain was, and then you were completely wrong or led down the wrong path?

IT MAKES the book worth reading to the end, to find out if your suspicions were right all along. Some argue that plot twists make the book only good for the first read, then ineffective for subsequent reads after that, but we disagree. We read a book twice at least - once to get the plot twist surprise for the first time, then again to see where the breadcrumbs were dropped. You interpret the characters in a different more enlightened way and see different sides to them. We like knowing the ending of a book sometimes because then we can enjoy the narrative on a different level. And if you think about it, how many movies have you watched over and over again even though you know the ending? We still enjoy the ending of **'The Sixth Sense'**, or **'The Usual Suspects'**, no matter how many times we've seen them, even though we know now what is going on. But there's more on plot twists later in this guide.

LASTLY, before we leave this genre bundle section, we want to look at book covers in our genre. You must have a cover that fits the codes and conventions of your genre, as readers can be merciless in their criticism.

IF YOUR COVER design doesn't fit the genre then readers will simply not pick up your book, because it looks nothing like what they like reading, in their opinion. Again, it is better to blend in here than stand out as it is an irrefutable fact of book publishing that readers DO judge a book by its cover.

IN THIS LAST SECTION, we will talk about what kinds of images and colours to use in your book cover design. We strongly recommend you hire a cover designer who understands your genre and knows what they are doing with your cover, as when authors design the cover themselves unfortunately they generally do look homemade and don't convey the message that the reader is expecting with crispness and clarity. In short, when put up against the leading lights in the genre they look amateurish and stick out like a sore thumb. A good cover designer need not be expensive, there are some very good designers to be found on sites like 99 designs and Fiverr, but the mantra to remember here is "you get what you pay for".

. . .

WHEN WE LOOKED at the top 50 crime books that are selling on Amazon, the same colours and themes stood out to us. We saw mysterious locations, dark blue, black, and red colours used in images and fonts, easy to read texts, straightforward font styles and just enough clarity in the images used for the reader to wonder what the meaning behind using that old, rickety shed or bleak-looking forest is. And, as we've said earlier, it's much better for your book cover to blend in amongst these than to stand out. In my early days of writing We used to think, "Oh, but if we designed a brightly coloured book, ours would stand out from all the others on the shelf." But then we quickly realised that this was for all the wrong reasons. Imagine all the books in the top 50 on your reader's bookshelf - and then yours amongst them. Would it look like it belonged or not? Then you'll know if you've hit the sweet spot of cover design. To be frank, if you design a cover that doesn't belong in the genre you are writing in then you will make your readers wonder about the quality of your writing and basically, if you've missed the design mark then you will have nothing in your book that they will want to read. Your readers won't take you seriously because, quite simply, you haven't taken your reader's requirements seriously. You can't expect to succeed with your book if you don't give your readers what they want and expect.

IN YOUR **'How to Write a Novel from Scratch'** you will see a selection of images that give the correct vibe of a thriller/crime genre book. Look at them closely. What elements in these images raise questions? What are the common elements? What mood do these images evoke? When you have a clear idea of the mood you want to evoke in your reader, gather together some images that create that mood and send them to your cover designer. They will then understand the look you are going for and design something that fits your genre. Get an expert in your chosen genre and you will not regret it. You can gather your images by going on a royalty-free site like Pixabay or Pixels, or by simply Googling words such as 'isolated cottage' or 'eerie woodland' and you will be immediately inspired. You start to wonder who lives in the cottage? Why have they moved there? Have they moved there because they used to live in a city? Or they got chucked out of the city? Did they commit a crime in the city and now they've been banished to this creepy, isolated cottage? Or are they living in that isolated cottage to get away from someone who was threatening them? You can see how the mind starts to race just from the simplest of ideas or images Write down all the ideas that spring to mind from your image search and circle the ones that stand out to you the most. This will help your cover designer to design the cover you can see in your head, and when you get the first draft of your brand new cover you will be thrilled.

So, let's conclude this section with a full rundown of our novel idea, using all the elements we have explored using **The Genre Bundle**:

The Talking Walls

A young girl, Sophie, is reported missing by her best friend, Alice.

The police investigate what looks like now to be a disturbing and chilling murder. Alice comes from a perfect family; her mother Meg and her construction worker father, Ben.

Sophie's family live on the outskirts of town in an isolated cottage.

When DCI Tom Nichols starts watching Alice's family more closely at Sophie's funeral, he realises not everything is as it seems, when he notices Alice's mother behaving suspiciously.

And her pointed silence on the murder - and her daughter's relationship with the victim - only serves to lead DCI Nichols to suspect her more - and adds to the sinister mystery of how Sophie came to die that day.

HERE WE HAVE a super compelling plan for either a psychological thriller, horror, mystery or a crime fiction book. We have adhered to the rules of the Top 50 Bestsellers on Amazon, so we know we are on the right lines for a successful novel.

4

Crime Books - Do's and Don't's

How to Write a Novel from Scratch - Workbook section 4

THIS SECTION IS PURELY PUT TOGETHER from all the things we have learned since we delved into the murky world of crime fiction writing. Along the way, we have made a lot of mistakes and learned the hard way from scathing reports back from our editor after the first draft of our manuscript for **'The Burying Place'**, our debut crime thriller novel. These mistakes were not made because we didn't care or were trying to cut corners or fool our audience. We had previously written three very successful and well-received novels, but in the historical fiction genre, which is massively different on every front to crime fiction. So, we had long flowing sentences, scenes that were described with gorgeous, but very "flowery" language, and lots of historical contexts which made the novel much longer than the traditional length of crime fiction novels. So, there were a lot of habits to change, which is exactly why researching the main **do's and don'ts** of the crime genre was helpful. So, this chapter is dedicated to giving you a selection of the best **do's and don'ts** that we have found from our research.

. . .

The full selection can be found in your 'How to Write a Novel from Scratch' workbook.

The first main thing to ensure you adhere to when writing crime fiction is you must grab your reader from the first chapter. This is something we call the 'wallop' scene - it wallops you and makes you take notice.

If you are setting the scene in a historical romance then you may use a long opening, using flowery prose as this hooks the reader differently. But crime fiction readers want to get thrown into the action, right into the murder/action scene and get their bearings from there. Think about the best crime drama you've ever seen - the BBC drama **'Line of Duty'** is brilliant at hooking in the viewer immediately. It's all blue lights and sirens as the opening credits roll, and technical lingo that you're not at all following but you are hooked because the actors are talking so convincingly in character that you are right there alongside them. The action progresses further with some kind of criminal bust scene with firearms officers and tactical response teams preparing to take down a threat or arrest a suspect. We know nothing about the crime yet, nothing about the reason the police are there, but we don't care. We just want action! Before you know it, as a viewer, you are twenty minutes in with more questions than answers. The screenwriter's job here is done! The best way to understand how this effect on the reader/viewer is achieved is to put yourself in their position. Think about what hooks you in and emulate that.

Including characters that are different and diverse also creates a world in which your reader will feel interested being in. Different personalities amongst your characters set up conflict - the young energetic new cop, the older disgruntled worn out soon-to-retire mentor, the sly villain who is rubbing everyone up the wrong way - and drive the narrative forward. Another reason to have a mixture of characters, personalities, ages, genders etc... is so the reader doesn't forget who everyone is in the story. This is very important when naming your characters. You shouldn't have Bill, Bob, Bernard, Beryl and Belinda all in the same story as these names are too similar sounding and the reader will need to picture them to follow their story. Jack, Max, Linda and Steve are easily distinguishable names, so will help your reader to follow their narratives.

ANOTHER GREAT TIP for what to do in your crime writing is to leave the reader wanting more. This doesn't necessarily just mean the cliff-hanger at the end of the novel. It means mini-cliff-hangers within the story. The best way we've seen this done in quite a few novels is to finish a chapter with a dilemma, or surprise, or mini-cliff-hanger including some kind of peril the character finds themselves in, then the next chapter starts in a different place with another character, then the following chapter we are back with the first character. That one-chapter break keeps the reader hooked as they have to read the chapter in between to get to the answer. Following this **ABABAB** rhythm in your story can build a strong narrative structure that will propel your reader into the thick of the action and towards the big finale where potentially both characters meet with the amazing discovery or the final showdown.

A MASSIVE THING that annoys the pants off readers is when the dialogue between characters just doesn't sound authentic. Now, this is a really hard thing to try to explain, because it is a *feeling* you get as a reader where you go, "mmm, that just doesn't sound like what that person would say in that situation." This is especially present when writing dialogue that children speak. We know writers want to convey the story, and the words they put in children's mouths have to do that sometimes, but hearing a child say, "that terrible man wearing the blue shirt and grubby trainers looked like he was going to get up to no good in that shop then mummy. I think we should call the police," just doesn't sound right. Little Billy is more likely to say, "Mum, that creepy weirdo is doing creepy stuff and freaking me out." Writers shouldn't shoehorn a clumsy description in here, as the child simply wouldn't notice specifics like that unless directly asked. The description can be added in perhaps when the parent looks over at them. So, don't be afraid to *think like a child* when writing dialogue for them. They are very short and to the point, with primal desires for chocolate and speak monosyllabically most of the time.

REFLECT this in your writing to sound authentic.

THROWING in a load of red herrings is also a tried and tested way of keeping your readers hooked on your crime novel. They want to show off by guessing whodunnit, so if you can keep them guessing for as long as possible with lots of potential suspects then do so. But make sure each new suspect has a *reason* to be a suspect. If the reader gets to the end of the novel and the killer isn't who they expected it to be, but someone completely different then they have to have been bread-crumbed into the story so their guilt is plausible. There's nothing worse as a reader to have a group of suspects in mind, then to find out it's the cousin that no one knew about and who only turned up in the last chapter. You know what I'm talking about, right?

MAKE IT HARD TO GUESS, not impossible, otherwise, you'll receive a salty review.

PUTTING in a great level of detail into your descriptions is an excellent way of helping your reader visualise the scene, weather, characters and the emotion in the scene. A detailed description of the hairs rising on the back of a tanned arm, the twitch in a blue eye, and the motionless stare of one character as they look over at the thing that scares them the most, can bring your reader into the story and ensure they focus on nothing else other than your narrative.

BEFORE YOU THROW your main character into a terrible predicament, you must ensure that you have given your reader enough reason to *like* them. No one will care about a perilous situation that befalls the main character if they haven't forged an affinity with them. So you must include establishing scenes at the start of your novel that includes the main character and elements of their life that make them human, likeable and worth your support and hopes for a positive outcome for them. Include scenes where they are with their family, or have something to work towards regaining, a scene with their pet that shows their softer side etc...

FINALLY, one of the main things that crime writers need to do to make their readers have complete faith in their writing is to make sure that all the police procedures in their novel are accurate.

THERE IS nothing worse when reading a crime novel than to feel that the procedures when arresting suspects and interviewing them aren't accurate. It makes the reader lose faith in the novel, as if these details aren't accurate then the writer hasn't put the effort in to make them so. You can guarantee that the reader of crime novels will no doubt be amateur sleuths themselves and watch all the police dramas on the TV. So your sloppy mistake with the reading of a suspects rights will stand out like a sore thumb to them. The best thing you can do, and it's something we have done in our crime novels, is to hire an expert in the field you are writing about and ask them to be a beta reader for you.

BETA READERS ARE people who read the first version of your novel and give you honest feedback on whether they liked it, it made sense and if there are any plot holes.

WORDS TO THE WISE, it is best to drop any ego you have with this step as this is invaluable advice and if you don't take it on board you will no doubt see it resurface in a less than favourable review of your novel - and by then it is too late to do anything about it, your mistake is there for all to see. For our novels, we asked a fellow writer, and ex-Met police detective, Mark Romain, to read our novels and tell us if there was anything that wasn't accurate in the police procedures throughout. He did so and it made the novel so much richer and accurate.

OUR REVIEWS HAVE REFLECTED this and we are so glad we found Mark and took this important step.

YOU WILL FIND MANY, many more good tips for what to do and not do in your **'How to Write a Novel from Scratch'** workbook, and also a section where you can add in your own as and when you come across them.

NEXT, WE COME ON TO 'ENDINGS' - which is a strange place to put it at this point in the guidebook. It will all make sense as we proceed.

5

Endings

How to Write a Novel from Scratch - Workbook section 5

WHEN IT COMES TO **ENDINGS**, novel writers tend to fall into one of two camps - they know exactly how to end their story, or they haven't got a clue.

THE FIRST GROUP more than likely have based their story around the cool ending that has been floating around their head for ages, and then piece the narrative around leading up to this conclusion. The second group of writers - usually "pantsers" if we're being completely honest (and that's fine to write like this if that is your natural style) - tend to start strongly with their story but then start to fade around halfway in as their ideas dry up and they lose their way without some kind of structure to follow.

THIS SECTION on endings will help both camps - add extra ideas to the pot of the writers with a nugget of an idea, and those writers with no clue where their story is going.

. . .

Readers want a good ending. That's what the point is of reading, right? They've paid out money for your book and don't want to spend hours reading it only to find their efforts have been wasted by a lame ending that doesn't satisfy or even worse one that doesn't suit the lead-up or tie up loose ends.

In your **'How to Write a Novel from Scratch'** workbook you will see in the **Endings** section a checklist of the different types of endings your story can have.

Below is a summary of the elements of each.

A happy ending is when the main character achieves their goal. You can look in your character descriptions and a basic plan to see what this goal was at the beginning of your ideas stage or refer to any notes you have made elsewhere. This ending makes everyone (apart from the villain of the story) happy. It's a 'feel-good' ending.

The sad ending is the tragic ending. Your main character fails at their mission. People die and everything goes wrong. But there is another way of looking at this type of ending - could your main character have learned a lesson? Even though it was a sad ending, could they have learned a personal thing about themselves in that mission? Or could your sad ending be where the main character achieves their mission, but it doesn't end how they wanted to and why. For example, a police officer finds the killer, arrests the killer - so he's **achieved his original mission,** but the killer wriggles free and throws himself under a bus. The story doesn't end how the police officer wants it to as now the victim's family won't get justice. Sad endings can be less than traditional, and open to interpretation as to what the word 'sad' means. Again, these are just examples of ideas to get your creative juices flowing.

ANOTHER TYPE of ending is when the main character **fails at the mission**, but he learns what he needed to learn about himself by the end of the story. Even though the police officer from our previous example caught the killer, he didn't bring him to justice how he wanted to - but did he realise the handcuffs weren't on properly which enabled the killer to escape? So the police officer learns from this mistake for next time - if there's a sequel? This is something to look out for in sequels. How are past mistakes rectified and atoned for in the next films in the chapter? Marvel films are good at doing this.

THE **FULL CIRCLE ending** is an ending that brings the readers back to the setting or situation that the characters started in, but things have changed for them. The main character may have either learned a lesson and become a changed person with a different and improved outlook on life. The Tom Hanks movie **'The News of the World'** is an excellent example of this type of ending. Hanks' character starts as quite a lonely person, travelling from town to town to read newspapers to the townsfolk, many of whom cannot read. It is their only window to the outside world and he commands large audiences each time he arrives in a new place. After he meets a young orphan girl and takes her under his wing, he becomes a changed person and finally by the end of the movie he is more contented in his life now he has a companion in the young girl, who teaches him that he can open his heart and doesn't have to travel alone. She becomes his daughter and helps him read the news to the towns they visit, and both become fulfilled by their life together. Same beginning scenes, same end scenes in terms of locations but much has changed in their lives along the journey. The premise of the story is that he has to the young girl to the safety of the only family she has left, but when he finds them he realises that they are not right for her and decided to go back for her. He realises that his happiness and fulfilment relies on his bond with this young girl - and the same goes for her. By the end of the movie, both characters are changed for the better and safe with each other. Technically, Hanks fails in his mission but achieves an even better goal.

THE **BIG SHOCK** ending is pretty self-explanatory. Disaster movies are great at these types of endings. Who else thought that the asteroid would miss earth in the film **'Deep Impact'**? But no, it hits and takes out half the planet, but the real moral of the story is how we adapt in the worst circumstances imaginable. Some will make it, some won't. the big shock is that we still believe it will miss earth (like its sister movie **'Armageddon'** released in the same year. The big shock ending is a great type of ending, as long as it is used carefully. If you kill off a loved character without a good reason then you are going to make a lot of readers unhappy. However, if you do it right then you will make them go "wow!" J.K. Rowling is great at **big shock** endings - think Severus Snape, Albus Dumbledore, Cedric Diggory and even poor old Dobby the House Elf! Who saw *that* coming in the books?! But heartbreaking though it is, these endings are brilliant at drawing in the reader.

BIG SHOCK ENDINGS can also include plot twists, which make the shock even more effective. Think of **'Primal Fear'** starring Richard Gere and Edward Norton, and also **'The Usual Suspects'** with Kevin Spacey. These endings are completely unexpected and we have to admit, we never saw them coming, hence why they are still to this day two of our favourite films. Why? because the ending completely drew us in. The first rule of thumb with any writing is that if you emulate a style you personally like then there is a good chance your reader will like it too.

THE **CLIFFHANGER** ENDING works especially well if you have another book coming soon in the series. You will make the reader want to buy your next book because they will be keen to find out what happens next. In our first book in the Rachel Morrison detective series, **'The Burying Place'** the final line reads, *"I know what you did. But don't worry, it's our little secret."* Rachel then looks around to see who is watching her but can't see anyone - but someone from the book knows what she's done and she fears her secret will come out, giving her reason to panic. But the book ends there and you have to read the next book, **'We Don't Speak About Mollie'** and the rest of the series to find out what Rachel does about this threat.

Essentially, you want your book to create excitement in the reader to get the next instalment to your book series, which means more revenue for you.

Think of your habits.

When you find a writer you love (for us it's C.J. Sansom and his **Shardlake Series** of books) your readers want your next book the minute it goes on pre-order. J.K. Rowling at the height of her **Harry Potter series** fame had midnight releases where die-hard Potter fans queued up outside bookshops and supermarkets late at night waiting for midnight to strike on release day and swarmed the huge pallets of crisp, fresh books that were wheeled out.

Quote from co-author, Claire Hackney:

"I remember it well as I was one of those fans queuing up in my wizard hat for my copy of the Order of the Phoenix. I'd enjoyed the previous book, the Goblet of Fire so much that I couldn't wait to find out what happened next between Harry and Lord Voldemort. J.K. Rowling is a master at the cliffhanger ending. You just NEED to know what happens next in the lives of Harry, Ron and Hermione."

SOME READERS HATE CLIFFHANGER endings when they are crudely done. This is when a writer will deliberately want to cash in on readers buying the next book by essentially only writing half a book, or splitting one big book into two. Never do this. It's obvious to hardened readers what you are doing and to be honest it's pretty lame to do this. You won't win fans of your writing if you disrespect them in this way. A cliffhanger ending should be done subtly and when the ending of the book is still satisfying in its own right, but with the added menace of a loose end - may be a surviving villain or a piece of the puzzle still not found/solved. The way to do cliffhanger endings well is simple - tie up 99% of all plot lines and story elements, but leave one thing back from being completely resolved. Leave one tiny morsel, one little breadcrumb for the readers to come back for next time. Dangle a little clue, a little light in the darkness, a step not taken, a question left unanswered. Do this and you will keep fans coming back for more each time.

A **FUNNY OR humorous ending** can also be a feel-good ending to your book. After all the trials and tribulations, heartaches and achievements in the narrative, an uplifting, light-hearted, funny ending will give the reader a smile of accomplishment when they read the last page. There's no more need for dramatic twists and turns, our hero(ine) has achieved the impossible and saved the day. You as the writer have decided against a cliffhanger ending (your readers have been through enough already, right?) so you give them one last laugh to make them close the cover with a smile. Your main character, who has a propensity to trip over his shoelaces for example does so but this time it leads into the arms of the princess, who smiles and shakes her head knowingly. Our hero(ine) smiles ruefully and shrugs. Think of the characters in your story, their quirks, their traits, their personalities, their journey travelled. What lessons have they learned? What funny, goofy quirk is still there in them, even though they have fought off dragons and monsters from the village?

A **HIGHLY EMOTIONAL** ending where it's really when you pull on your reader's heartstrings. It could be happy, it could be sad, it could be tragic. What do they care about at this point in the narrative? Does someone they care about die in tragic but heroic circumstances? Again, our thoughts drift to poor old Dobby the House Elf. We are not ashamed to admit we sobbed our hearts out at the end of **The Deathly Hallows**, and if anyone reading this didn't dissolve into a puddle at the end of **Titanic** then we'll be very surprised. How many times have you been scared to turn the page because it's not looking good for your favourite character's chances in the final battle? Alternatively, who has found themselves crying with happy tears when their favourite character against all odds wins the girl/boy through sheer guts and determination? Either way, highly emotional endings are excellent devices to satisfy your reader. After all, emotion sells. And if it's good enough for William Shakespeare (who knew a thing or two about highly emotional endings to his plays) then it's good enough for us mere mortals.

ANOTHER TYPE of ending is a **reflective ending.** Similar to the full-circle ending, this ending involves the main character learning hard lessons throughout the narrative, growing up in experience and then going on to do good with it in the next book, or part of their life. This evolution of the character can be planned into their character arc (more on this later). So, a reflective ending is a more vocalised version of the full circle, but the main character communicates this change in their view on the world and their actions more to the other characters in the narrative. "I'm a changed man, Debbie. I'm going to make something of my life from now on" and so on...

THE FINAL TYPE of ending we will outline in this section is the **quote** ending. This type of ending involves a quote your main character said at the beginning of the book which now, by the end of the book makes sense. It could be a principle they live by, a family motto or something is written in a language that the character didn't understand until now after the events of the story have unfolded. or something they live on now makes sense, and they say the last few words where it has more meaning. So, it could be something where it's a principle that they live by.

TAKE THE MOVIE, **'A River Runs Through It'**. At the start, the family are very happy, very together and look after each other. But then the character Paul, played by Brad Pitt gets involved with the wrong crowd and starts to develop self-destructive habits. Eventually the family split. The narrator, voiced by Robert Redford says at the end of the movie, "and then a river runs through it..." and all that has happened in the movie begins to make sense - making this line, and the title of the movie pack a punch.

So, now we've covered all of the different types of endings, and hopefully, your creative juices are flowing with ideas for your novel, go to the section in your **'How to Write a Novel from Scratch'** workbook where there is space for you to write down your favourite two or three types of endings.

Free-write all the ideas you have in your head, and as always DON'T edit yourself at this stage. Start to rotate all the characters in your plan to where they all face some kind of ending to see which ones spark off ideas in your head. There is space in your workbook to jot down your three best ideas and flesh them out more. You could even combine elements of a couple of endings - there are no rules at this point, it's whatever you feel is best for your characters and plotline.

Let's take a moment to track back and see how far we've already come in our novel planning. We have our basic ideas from our Fiction Square. We have a title, we have our character names and roles, words for our blurb, a couple of locations for our main scenes, some power words to strengthen our narrative, an idea of an appropriate word count for our crime novel and also a writing schedule timeframe. We also have a great insight into the dos and don'ts of writing crime novels. Now, added to all this excellent information, we have a vast selection of different types of endings for our novel.

Our novel is beginning to take shape and taking on all the elements that will make it a compelling read. Let's add an ending idea here:

The Talking Walls

A young girl, Sophie, is reported missing by her best friend, Alice.

The police investigate what looks like now to be a disturbing and chilling murder. Alice comes from a perfect family; her mother Meg and her construction worker father, Ben.

Sophie's family live on the outskirts of town in an isolated cottage.

When DCI Tom Nichols starts watching Alice's family more closely at Sophie's funeral, he realises not everything is as it seems, when he notices Alice's mother behaving suspiciously.

And her pointed silence on the murder - and her daughter's relationship with the victim - only serves to lead DCI Nichols to suspect her more - and adds to the sinister mystery of how Sophie came to die that day.

How ABOUT THE ending being a highly emotional one:

DCI Tom Nichols dies in the final fight with the murderer but saves the person who was to become the next victim.

YOU MIGHT THINK this type of ending has been done a million times, but it has only been done once with your story idea and you writing it. There is no such thing as an original idea anymore, only original ways of telling it.

6

How Many Characters Will I Need?

How to Write a Novel from Scratch - Workbook section 6

THE NEXT LESSON we're going to talk about is, **How many characters will I need?** To be frank about it, there is no specific answer to this, it does depend on the type of novel you are planning to write. If your protagonist is a lone wolf working their way through an apocalyptic world there is a great chance they will not come into contact with a lot of other people on the journey, but if your story involves a World Cup chasing football team working their way through the games up to the final, then there will be more characters to involve in the narrative.

REGARDLESS OF HOW many you have, there is a basic list of character roles that readers will expect to see in your novel. These include a protagonist (your main character), an antagonist (the "villain" of the story - not always human, it could be a different type of entity all together such as the landscape or weather), the main character's ally (the friend that assists them in the story), the antagonist's ally, the person or thing that needs "saving", and the person or thing that acts as the main character's voice of reason.

For example: In **'Harry Potter and the Philosopher's Stone'**, the characters are as follows:

Protagonist = Harry Potter

Antagonist = Lord Voldemort (in whatever form he appears in - no spoilers here!)

Protagonist's Ally/confidante = Ron Weasley/Hermione Granger

Person/thing that needs saving = Hogwarts School of Witchcraft and Wizardry and all who reside within. You can include the wider world too as the plot moves on. You could also double up here with Harry being the victim of Voldemort and vice versa

Protagonist's voice of reason = Albus Dumbledore

In your **'How to Write a Novel from Scratch'** workbook you will find space to jot down your character types as part of your novel planning. In those pages, you will also find the heavy lifting has been done for you as we have written a long list of stock character traits you can refer to to help you to flesh out your characters further.

Aim to pick a couple of traits from the list for each character. Remember that even the best heroes and worst villains have light and shade, so don't pick three bad for the villain and three good for the hero.

Mix it up a bit.

Not all heroes are good ALL the time and not all villains are bad ALL the time. Some of the greatest villains in history have certain good qualities, such as courage, intelligence and wit for example. Likewise, some of the greatest heroes have bad qualities, such as arrogance, violence and jealously. It's these flaws that make us love them, or loath them, but ultimately empathise with them and their humanity and realness.

Let's look at our story and our main characters and add some traits —

The Talking Walls

A young girl, Sophie, is reported missing by her best friend, Alice.

The police investigate what looks like now to be a disturbing and chilling murder. Alice comes from a perfect family; her mother Meg and her construction worker father, Ben.

Sophie's family live on the outskirts of town in an isolated cottage.

When DCI Tom Nichols starts watching Alice's family more closely at Sophie's funeral, he realises not everything is as it seems, when he notices Alice's mother behaving suspiciously.

And her pointed silence on the murder - and her daughter's relationship with the victim - only serves to lead DCI Nichols to suspect her more - and adds to the sinister mystery of how Sophie came to die that day.

Character traits:

Sophie is poor, dressed in hand-me-downs and very quiet

Alice is well-spoken, well-dressed, polite and confident

Meg is well-spoken, attractive and competent in her job

Ben is highly skilled and hard-working

DCI Tom Nichols is jaded, tired, scarred by his past but has a backbone of steel and is tenacious

BY THIS POINT we may also have a physical description of the main characters, so jot that down too as you start to get to know your novel characters.

7

Characters - Part 1

How to Write a Novel from Scratch - Workbook section 7

NOW WE HAVE WORKED on what traits our main characters have, we will now look at how to build our characters further.

THE FIRST STAGE is to take each character one by one and think about their one **dominant trait.** This could be they are brave, they are angry, or even that they are bereaved.

MAIN CHARACTER NAME: ....
• DOMINANT TRAIT?

• ONE EXAMPLE OF WHAT THIS TRAIT LOOKS LIKE:

• WHAT WOULD BE AN OPPOSITE TRAIT TO THIS?

• WHAT DOES THIS TRAIT LOOK LIKE?

We can then consider what the *opposite* to this trait would be and how *that* trait would come across in the narrative.

By DOING this for each character you will start to **build the arc** of each character, enhancing the narrative. We will cover character arcs in a later chapter but a basic definition of a character arc is the journey they go on throughout the narrative and how their characteristics change from the beginning to the end. So, a character who starts off as arrogant and selfish may have events happen to him in the story which humble him and by the end, he realises the benefits of being more down to earth and selfless.

THIS PERSONAL JOURNEY the character travels in the story is what makes the book or film worth watching. Lessons are learned by the characters and we as readers feel uplifted and inspired for being part of this journey.

IN THE CHARACTERS **Part 1** section of your **'How to Write a Novel from Scratch'** workbook there is space for you to write in your character traits for each main player in your narrative (including the main character, their ally, their confidante, the antagonist and their ally), examples of these traits, the opposite of these traits and what these traits look like. Try and think of as many traits as will fit the idea in your head that you have for your character as this will help lots as you are fleshing your characters out in **Characters Part 2** - the next chapter in your workbook which we will come on to next.

Let's look at our example story and the main character.

DCI Tom Nichols – his dominant trait is that he is tenacious in his investigative style, sometimes to his detriment as he gets reprimanded by his boss sometimes for breaking the rules.

Below is an example of how this could be shown in the story -

> **DCI Nichols is called into the boss's office after a complaint is lodged from a witness he interviewed. However, this interview created chatter between the suspects leading to a valid reason to obtain a search warrant. This drives the plot forward but gives our protagonist a "final warning" from his superiors, which adds to the stakes in the narrative.**

Let's now consider what the opposite of this trait could be -

> **DCI Tom Nichols is carefree, almost blasé about the investigations he undertakes, therefore leading to being a timid and mild detective chief inspector and never ruffling any feathers.**

Wow, how boring would this story be if we used the opposite of this tenacious trait? Bit by imagining the opposite, you can see how good your dominant trait is, reassuring you as the writer that you have made a good decision. No one likes a nice, perfect detective, right?

8

Characters - Part 2

How to Write a Novel from Scratch - Workbook section 8

IN THIS SECTION we will look at the dominant trait that each of your characters has in their personality, and how that can be shown in your narrative. We will also add to this dominant trait a couple of other traits to help us decide if that makes them good or bad. The purpose of doing this is to flesh out each character and make sure they are all individuals within the story and that there is a real reason for them to be taking up space in your narrative. **Every character has to have a reason to be there,** otherwise, the reader will think *what is the point of them* in the story and how on earth did they make the final cut if they are so watery that they carry out no function or progress the story in any way.

IN YOUR WORKBOOK, there is space in **Characters Part 2** to fill in your ideas. If your character is good then pick 2 good traits and 1 bad trait for them to have. This process makes them human.

. . .

REVERSE this if your character is bad (2 bad traits, 1 good). In each box write an example of how you would show this in your narrative. There is space to do this step for five individual characters, which is enough for the main players in your story.

TRY TO IMAGINE what star sign your character is. This could inform your decisions on what character traits they have. For example, is your character a fiery Aries? Or a duplicitous Gemini? Or a hard-shelled, tough Cancer? Whether you buy into astrology or not, character stereotypes do exist and star signs often give individuals in novels quite specific personality traits.

ALSO, consider your character's family background. Are they from a broken home? Are they an only child? Have they been orphaned? These huge life experiences can significantly affect a character's personality and give you a lot of meat to put on the bones of each. Other things to think about with character traits is if your character is wealthy, poor, educated or not. What hobbies do they have? Are they good at them? What kind of a person does this make them? Is one of their character traits that they hate heights? What impact could that have in the story if they are faced with a life or death decision at 30,000 feet? Do they volunteer at the local old folks' home? Are they afraid of anything?

THINK about what their dreams were as a child. Was it to travel the world but they are too scared to spend the money on a ticket because they have a family who depends on them. What if they won the lottery in your story? Would they fulfil their lifelong dream then or spend it on something less personal/selfish? What is their Achilles heel that having a lot of money all of a sudden would exacerbate? Are they a drinker? A gambler? Take the film **'Back To The Future'**. Marty McFly's Achilles heel comes out whenever somebody, mainly Biff Tannen (in his younger guise) calls him "chicken".

Whenever he hears this word, Marty is incapable of rising above it and loses his cool, which puts him in grave peril.

OR WHAT ABOUT IN the Harry Potter books whenever anyone says anything derogatory to Harry about his parents. Take the scene in **'Harry Potter and the Prisoner of Azkaban'** when horrible old Aunt Marge criticises Harry's mother, Lily, therefore angering Harry to the point where he cannot control his magical powers and blows her up like a balloon. Although Harry knows he cannot perform magic outside the walls of Hogwarts before his 17th birthday, he cannot help himself thus finding himself in trouble with the Ministry of Magic. His love and loyalty to his family and friends are Harry's dominant traits, but also his Achilles heel, which gives his character light and shade and in turn makes him a thoroughly interesting character.

BY CONSIDERING CHARACTER TRAITS, and developing our ideas about which is the dominant trait, we are making our characters multi-dimensional. This keeps the reader interested throughout. They want to follow the progress and evolution of your character, which can be very lucrative for you if, like J.K. Rowling you decide to include your characters in a full series of books your readers will become obsessed with.

So, if we look at our story, our main character, **DCI Tom Nichols'** Achilles heel could be:

He cannot help himself when he senses injustice or some kind of cover-up. This occurs when he reports the father of Alice, Ben, to the fraud investigation team when he finds out Ben has faked a credit card receipt to give him an alibi for the night Sophie died.

THIS ACHILLES HEEL teamed up with his dominant trait of being tenacious, causes him to ruffle even more feathers and start to sound as if he has a vendetta against the main suspect of Ben. Our story is developing nicely and gathering pace.

9

Character Quirks

How to Write a Novel from Scratch - Workbook section 9

OUR NEXT FOCUS as we build our book from scratch is **Character Quirks**. Quirks are the little idiosyncrasies that individuals in life have, and these are great to add into our character descriptions as they serve to set each character apart from the next and make them interesting. The main thing to remember when considering character quirks is that they make sense for the character we are building and that they stay consistent throughout the story or series. So, if your character likes his coffee black then he has to have it black every time unless there is a specific reason in the story why this changes. Believe me, readers will notice if things just change without good reason. If you want your reader to be thoroughly invested in your story then you must help them to get to know and love/loathe your characters as if they knew them in real life.

IN YOUR **'How to Write a Novel from Scratch'** workbook there are several pages for you to use when planning the character quirks of each main player in your story. On these pages, you can write in some character quirks for each of the main players in your story.

Think about why this quirk is relevant to your character, and also a potential scene where this quirk could be shown in their actions or speech.

THE MAIN THING TO remember here is to show, don't tell. This is a much better way of communicating to the reader your character's quirk. It is lazy storytelling to say, *"Adam felt angry so he frowned."* Much better to say, *"Adam's forehead creased when he heard what Grace said. His fists clenched around the rope leaving his knuckles white."* This second description allows the reader to picture the actions, whereas the first description just tells the reader what emotion triggered the action.

THERE IS space in your **Character Quirks** section of your **'How to Write a Novel from Scratch'** workbook for two character quirks per character so have a good think about what they will be and why they make sense for the character you are building. If you are stuck on ideas there are five pages of possible quirks at the end of this section for you to choose from. Hopefully, this will get the juices flowing.

THE NEXT FEW pages of the workbook will give you a long list of character weaknesses, also known as negative traits. Here you can decide what less-than-favourable quirks your characters will have. Like we have already discussed, every individual has elements of light and shade on their character make-up, so it is important to include good and bad traits. But remember, even Mr or Mrs Perfect has some traits deep down that add a little salt to that sugar. Otherwise, there is simply no character arc and in effect, no conflict in the story, which means your reader will switch off.

IF WE LOOK BACK at **DCI Tom Nichols,** we can add in a few character quirks for him too. Even though he is tenacious in his work, let's make him forgetful when it comes to personal appointments, meeting up with his on-off girlfriend, paying his council tax, that kind of thing? These negative traits can give our character some light and shade elements.

As a bonus to your character-building including quirks, we have included an extensive list of clichéd quirks to avoid.

A villain twirling their moustache and cackling "mwah-ha-haaa" is so old hat it belongs in the 1900s in those old black and white movies that include a damsel in distress being tied to a railway line by an unscrupulous pantomime villain, complete with mime hands. It has no place in a cutting edge, gritty crime drama where you desire your characters to be subtle and brooding. Likewise, a dirty vagrant scratching their backside and picking their nose is a little too overt in its description to satisfy our 21st Century reader. Think of it yourself. How many times have you groaned when you are introduced to a character in the story who is a clean-freak germaphobe, or someone who talks so fast that no one can follow because they are excited about something. Now, we fully understand that you are now probably thinking, "but that is exactly how these emotions would be communicated so why can't we use them?" We're not saying you can't, We're suggesting that you shouldn't just head straight for those clichéd, ham-fisted descriptions when you could be a little more subtle. Give your readers characters that they have seen before but are described more originally. For example, yes have a clean-freak in your story, but rather than having them moan and whinge to their guests that they are making a lot of mess, have your character subtly straighten a cushion while they are speaking, or invite their guests to drink their red wine in the kitchen avoiding the white cotton couch covers in the lounge. Remember to use show, not tell to make your character building even sharper. This is especially effective if you are planning a character shift in a plot twist at the end of your story. Your reader won't see it coming head-on if you temper your character quirks subtly, but will see it clear as day if your DNA-less crime scene coincides with a suspect that shaves his head and wears gloves all the time because he's a germaphobe.

Now we are getting to the really interesting part with our character building. We can now move on to the next part where we create extended character descriptions.

10

Extended Character Descriptions

How to Write a Novel from Scratch - Workbook section 10

IN THIS SECTION, we are going to write out full descriptions of our main characters. This is where our characters start to take shape as the flesh starts to be put on their bones. The aim here with this section is to start to get to know your characters inside and out. We are going to create their family history/tree, how they fit into the story, what job they do, their star sign, their hobbies, their strengths and their weaknesses. We will also think about what fears and vulnerabilities the character has and how that impacts their life.

DREAMS, obstacles and what the character's Achilles heel is are also vital components of building a character.

THINK of what would devastate this character, such as the loss of a loved one. The focus of the narrative could then be the aftermath of this tragedy and how that character copes and progresses. This also ties into what motivations the character has. What is propelling the character to the next goal they have in life? What propels them forward? Love? Revenge? To settle a score? Jot down some options in this section of your workbook to get a feel for the inner workings of your character.

THINK about what the character needs to learn in life and what happens if they don't. How does this character feel about it and why? Is this skill completely alien to them, but crucial to saving the world? What could be the worst thing to happen to them? Is it if their child was kidnapped? Or if they were an introvert then someone in a restaurant decided to storm over to them and fling the table from underneath them and challenge them to a fight. What would your character do in this extreme situation? How would they react? Think about your character's pet hates? What are their dark secrets? What would happen if these were revealed?

AS YOU WORK through each page in this section you will add an extra layer to your character. You will no doubt already have a picture in your head of what they look like but now you can build up a mental picture of their personality to go with their appearance.

THE REASON for building detailed character descriptions is so you can plan to change and evolve these characters throughout the narrative, thus creating the character arc. In Celeste Ng's novel **'Little Fires Everywhere'** the main character Elena Richardson starts off as the perfect housewife and mother. She is smartly dressed, perfectly coiffed and approaches every situation, however trying, with poise and grace, leading Mia Warren and her daughter Pearl to think that their own enigmatic lives are somewhat inferior. As the action in the novel plays out we discover that Elena is less than perfect, and her life changes considerably to where, by the end of the novel, she is dishevelled and simply clad in previously unthinkable sweat pants, her hair unkempt and dull.

. . .

Your extended character descriptions can help to create scenes in your head for your novel and help it to take shape. So, if there is a situation where your character needs to show his softer side, and his vulnerability and worst fears, you could have him lose someone important to him. This allows you to drive the narrative forward with a strong, emotional scene, and add in an impact scene (how it affects the character in their actions) to the story.

There is space in your **'How to Write a Novel from Scratch'** workbook to plan out an **Extended Character Description** for one character, but there is nothing to stop you from photocopying this section for as many characters as you want to use it for.

We now move on to going off the page with our characters and start to freestyle our ideas a bit more. This stage is really fun as it gives us the chance to properly open up the taps on our creativity.

11

Character Freestyle Points

How to Write a Novel from Scratch - Workbook section 11

IN THIS SECTION, we are going to look at how to freestyle write descriptions of our characters. This method of writing enables you to write everything you can think of without editing and pausing to second guess yourself. It is a pure writing purge. So, in your **'How to Write a Novel from Scratch'** workbook, there are four pages for you to pick your four main characters - we would suggest you choose your protagonist (main character), your antagonist (the villain), your protagonist's ally, and the person who needs saving. If the 'person who needs saving' is a thing or entity or natural event, the earth for example, then you could substitute this for the ally of the antagonist, if that person is a strong enough presence in your novel idea to justify their place. Alternatively, this fourth place could be taken by a joint protagonist if, say, it is a detective duo investigating a murder.

. . .

In your workbook, you will see that each **Character Freestyle Points** section has space to write in the character's name. Even if you haven't finalised your decision just yet put a name in here that you can mull over, so you don't forget. Then take a look at the stimulus ideas in the space below it. These are specifically written to generate ideas and get your thoughts out of your head.

Think about who your character is. What are their hopes and dreams for the future? What kinds of situations would make them angry, sad, happy or feel nothing. If your character was placed in these situations how would they react? What actions would they take? Something that we always think about when fleshing out characters is how they would react in day-to-day mundane situations. This can tell you a lot about a person and their inner character and integrity. Take for example when a character is driving his car. How does he drive it? Fast? Slow? Does he roar away from the traffic lights as soon as he sees the red and amber lights? Does he wait until both are replaced by a bold green light? Does he screech around corners ten minutes late for his appointment or does he drive five miles per hour below the speed limit and arrive with half an hour to spare to find the perfect parking space?

Think about your character's manners. How polite are they to waiters and desk clerks? How do they interact with the police force? If they are kind and considerate, does that mean they are uninteresting? Or are they like that as a cover for their real personalities? The possibilities are endless, but keep in mind that all character idiosyncrasies must stay consistent with that character throughout unless something in the plot changes this and the character evolves their personality because of these events.

Once you have filled in your four pages we can move on to the next and final part of the character-building section of our workbook - character arcs.

12

Character Arcs

How to Write a Novel from Scratch - Workbook section 12

A **CHARACTER ARC** IS, in a nutshell, the transformation of the character from the beginning of your story to the end. It tracks the journey they go on, how they evolve and what challenges these events present to them throughout the narrative.

BEFORE WE GET STUCK into character arcs for our characters we must first clarify the three-act structure of a story.

ACT 1 - THE BEGINNING. This is where we are introduced to the main character(s). there is an inciting event (something that kicks off the action and gives the protagonist the "first problem". We are introduced to the main elements of the story.

ACT 2 - THE MIDDLE. Here we lead on to the first "change". This could be a character change or an event change. For example, an event could change the life/opinion/goal of the protagonist to the point where the story changes direction. A problem is introduced to the story which sets off a chain of events that the protagonist has to solve. The middle is where the main action occurs, setting up the finale where all hell breaks loose.

ACT 3 - THE END. This is the part where we find out *how* the characters have changed after the events have taken hold. All loose ends are tied up unless the story is gearing up to offer a cliffhanger ending, then most of the ends will be tied up save one or two lingering threads. The story works towards a big finale, ending on a high and giving the reader a satisfied smile as they close the cover of the book they have immersed themselves in for the last few hours/days/months.

SO NOW WE have established the elements of a story that are split over the three acts, we can start to decide how we spread out the character evolution over the three acts, thus creating a literal arc across them.

IN YOUR **'HOW TO Write a Novel from Scratch'** workbook you have six pages to use, taking one for each character, as by now you have no doubt thought of secondary and tertiary characters in your story that are solid and you want to flesh them out a bit more. Here's where you can do that.

EACH PAGE HAS a section where you can write how your character behaves in act 1 and why. Think about how they show this to the world and the people around them. So, if you are reading a crime thriller and your protagonist is a detective getting some heat at work from their chief inspector then start with this scene and the aftermath. Do they go into the meeting with their superior in a cocky, arrogant way, entering without knocking and moving the chair before sitting down in it uninvited? Or do they take a big deep breath before knocking on the door and entering with head bowed?

EACH EXAMPLE SETS up a different image of the 'first problem' that occurs in the story or gives us the aftermath of that problem. Use your character descriptions in this part to flesh out the situation. If you have invented your character to be nervous and shy then show this through their body movements and facial expressions. Whatever you do, don't write, **"Cooper was nervous about his meeting with the chief."** *Show* this. **"Cooper inhaled a large, deep breath, collected his racing thoughts and took one last look in the mirror to check his tie was straight before walking over to the chief's office door."** Notice at no point do we use an adverb here. He doesn't need to "slowly" or "nervously" walk for us to get across to the reader he is nervous.

WHEN YOU ARE nervous you breathe deeply to calm yourself. Cooper's actions here *show* his feelings.

CHARACTER ARCS ARE *vital* to any story. If a character stays the same throughout the narrative, with no movement, no direction, no confidence then there is no direction in the story. If the character isn't moved or changed by the events in the story then is it a story your reader wants to spend their time reading? It would be a monumentally boring book if nothing evolved. Even stories that stay in one singular place, or are quite static in their location, such as the film **'Panic Room', 'Phone Booth'** or even **'The Martian,'** where the characters remain in one place for the vast majority of the time. The difference is that throughout this the character evolves and changes. Their arc has peaks and troughs. We follow their highs, their lows, their failures and successes, and this is the crux of the story. The story is their story of courage in the face of adversity. The story is about how an individual copes under extreme stress and overcomes insurmountable pressure.

. . .

WE AS READERS love a story of triumph against all odds, especially when our hero has suffered throughout. The more extreme the arc the better the character. Harry Potter, William Wallace, any character played by our favourite action heroes (Bruce Willis, Matt Damon, Sigourney Weaver) all overcome the most impossible problems - defeating Lord Voldemort with a wand; fighting the English army with half the men; destroying a catastrophic asteroid with a "sling-shot-around-the-moon" manoeuvre and detonating a nuclear warhead in space; sowing seedlings to grow food on Mars, outwitting and annihilating a ruthless, merciless giant alien respectively - and save the day. But they all learn something about themselves and their strengths and weaknesses, prejudices and failures-the-first-time mentality. Harry doesn't defeat Lord Voldemort in the first book. It takes him several losses (battles and friends) to learn what it is that will finally see he-who-should-not-be-named off. The same with William Wallace. He won the battle of Stirling Bridge in 1297 on a crest of a wave from his compatriots but lost the Battle of Falkirk in 1298. It took a battle that occurred at Bannockburn after Wallace's grisly execution, led by Robert the Bruce, to finally win the Scottish people their freedom. Bruce Willis's character in the 1998 film **'Armageddon'**, Harry Stamper, takes several attempts and lots of failures finally to shatter the asteroid that is hurtling towards the earth on course to destroy it and all who dwell on it. Only after sacrificing his life, does he finally succeed in the mission. Matt Damon's character, Mark Watney, in **'The Martian'** doesn't grow a potato from the first seedling he sows. Likewise, with Sigourney Weaver's character, Ellen Ripley in the **'Alien'** films. She doesn't figure out how to kill the alien onboard her spaceship until the final battle. And even then, it takes a few sequels to finish the job. Our point is that characters, to become the characters readers will love and cheer for, do not succeed on their first attempt. It takes failures and learning from these to achieve their goal. And that is what forms the content of their character arc.

. . .

LET'S TAKE ANOTHER EXAMPLE.

A young girl who is too shy to show off her amazing singing talent will only sing in her bedroom when her parents are out.

THIS FORMS the content of our first act- Act 1.

ONE DAY she is overheard by a neighbour who compliments her and tells her she is good enough to sing on stage. We then move on to act two where there is a *change* in the character. This neighbour gives her the first boost of confidence and recommends that she try and sing in front of her mum. But the young girl tries this and hits a bum note. She panics and runs away, embarrassed. This introduces our first problem.

Now, the rest of the act involves the young girl and her mum working together with the neighbour on confidence-building where they can finally get her to perform in front of a larger audience, maybe with a record executive friend of the neighbour sitting in the back seats.

WE MOVE into the third and final act now where the young girl has learned enough about herself and built her confidence up enough to be able to stand on the stage in front of the crowd, including the record executive, and also her father who has never heard her sing who has secretly kept an interest in her from afar after divorcing the girl's mother. She must put on the performance of a lifetime, leading us to an epic finale and the ending leaving us on a massive high as she signs her first record deal.

. . .

THE CHARACTER ARC includes all the events and ups/downs that get the girl from her bedroom in the first act to the glittering stage in the final act. These such transformations don't happen overnight. There will be significant events that will be both positive and negative throughout the story that build her hopes up and knock them down, but the arc in the character is how she reacts to each up and down, and how she grows from these experiences. We end up at the end of the story with a completely different person than who we started with.

THIS IS NOT ALWAYS in a positive way. Some character arcs can take a nice, happy character and send them into a descent into hell where they lose their loved ones and everything they hold dear. Consider the film '**Mad Max**' (1979). The film starts in an idyllic way with a happy and contented Max Rockatansky spending time with his beautiful wife and baby son. But a tragedy destroys Max's perfect life and he begins a descent into pure emotion-driven and hate-fuelled revenge on the murderous and unrepentant biker gang responsible. Max loses everything in that one moment and spends the rest of the film, and sequels, in a quest for violence against the monsters who took it from him. This is Max's character arc, from happy to vengeful. But even though it takes a nice, happy character away from the audience, it replaces him with someone who has arguably more interesting and adrenaline-fuelled adventures than nice old Max would have given us.

CHARACTER NAME ....

ACT 1
HOW WILL THEY ACT?

HOW CAN I SHOW THIS?
(USE CHARACTER DESCRIPTIONS)

ACT 2
HOW WILL THEY ACT?

HOW CAN I SHOW THIS?
(USE CHARACTER DESCRIPTIONS AND INCLUDE FAILURES)

ACT 3
HOW WILL THEY ACT?

HOW CAN I SHOW THIS?
(USE CHARACTER DESCRIPTIONS)

13

Research

How to Write a Novel from Scratch - Workbook section 13

DOING the right **research** for your book can make or break it. Whether your main character is a brain surgeon based in New York City or a cattle rancher based in Texas, you need to be able to describe these people and places accurately and know enough about the day-to-day details of the profession your main character does.

ONCE YOU HAVE DECIDED upon your storyline and fleshed out your characters, how do you go about researching key areas for your book?

THE OBVIOUS ANSWER in this day and age is the good old internet. While not everything on the world wide web can be relied upon as verbatim, there are an awful lot of sites that can offer amazing information. This chapter in the **'How to Write a Novel from Scratch'** workbook gives you a vast array of places you can look for all the information you could want for your book.

. . .

FIRSTLY, you can simply type in the thing you want to research into a search engine, such as Google. For example, if you need to know how to describe a German world war two uniform then you can simply type this into Google Images. Or if you want to describe a small town in Chicago in the 1920s then again type this into the search bar and you will see loads of different options ripe for your imagination to run wild. You can also look at town planning maps of areas by looking on Google Earth or Google Maps. The author of the **'Fifty Shades of Grey'** series, E.L. James admits to never even visiting Seattle before basing her million-selling novel series there. She would research the locations in her books by looking at pictures on the internet of them, which is a very common approach to take.

WE'LL ADMIT, we have never been to Alabama, USA but we based our novel, **'Meet Me at 10'** there. We must have got it right though because one of our Alabama-born beta-readers, Jessie, read the book and recognised as she was reading places that she'd visited as a child.

ANOTHER SNEAKY WAY TO look at street views and neighbourhoods is to go on Estate Agents websites and look at houses for sale or rent in the area where your characters live.

ON RIGHTMOVE, for example, you can see pictures of the insides of houses, and the location where they are situated. You can look at a street view also allowing you to see what the neighbourhood is like. This is a rich buffet of potential ideas for your character's houses and neighbourhoods. Visually seeing houses on streets where your characters live can help you to find the vocabulary to describe what their front gardens look like, or what era their house was built in. When you look inside houses for sale or rent you can sometimes stumble upon a diamond - a house built in the era your story is set and also decorated how you imagine your characters would decorate it. Your scene descriptions will just flow when you write them.

TripAdvisor is a great website for reading what other travellers have thought of the places you want to include in your novel. Most of the time they are brutally honest and outline the finer details of the place, the culture, the cuisine and the hotels. They also upload photographs of their experience, which can help you to make your location descriptions a little bit different than the rest of the books out there set in the same town or city. Quora is another website that can offer great information. On this site you can ask a question about anything and look up a keyword or search term and tonnes of information is at your disposal. If you look under 'questions' you will be able to see all the questions people have asked related to a certain subject matter, which can help you if your question fits under this bracket.

YouTube is a great website to find almost anything. People upload thousands of videos a day on every conceivable subject, so there is a good chance that popping in a search term will bring up something useful to you.

Looking on the National Archives website can help with researching a novel set in the past. If you contact one of the archivists who work there they might also be able to assist you with specific questions. Hiring a historian is an investment worth making if your novel is set in a particular period, such as Egyptian, Tudor or Victorian times. It can save you a lot of time and effort to just hire a professional. You would give them a crib sheet of everything that you need to know for your novel to feel authentic to the reader and then they would set about researching these things for you.

. . .

WE HIRED someone to research the 1950s for us, giving her a long list of things to look up, such as food, styles of dress, music that was in the charts in each year, significant historical events, and other suchlike things. Then, when we were writing the novels in **'The Shona Jackson series'** we could cherry-pick items that made the storyline and narrative much more rich and enjoyable for the reader to help them immerse themselves in the era the novels were set.

HIRING a historian might not be cheap, but it is worth it if you are not confident about researching. Plus, any good historian worth their salt will have subscribed to all the useful services, such as Ancestry.com and FindYourPast.com, saving you money that way.

SEARCHING keywords on social media sites, such as Instagram and Twitter can help to cast your net far and wide with potential help for information. If you type in #policeofficer or #tudorhouse or #mexicanfood you will find loads of images and people with a similar interest to you. These are excellent fonts of knowledge to extend your knowledge of the subject you are researching. You can also see other people's photographs of certain locations you want to include in your novel.

ONE WAY of gathering information that often, strangely, gets overlooked is to simply talk to other people. Interview people you know who are experts in a certain field.

Quote from co-author, Claire Hackney:
"My dad is an electrical engineer, so if I need to know how to rewire something, or if an electrical circuit is the cause of a major incident in my storyline then I will speak to my dad and ask him to talk me through how this would work, what wires go where and repercussions of short circuits etc... His technical know-how transcends to computer hardware too, so if I have a computer geek in my novels

then my prose and dialogue sound authentic when this character interacts with others."

FOR OUR DETECTIVE Rachel Morrison series of novels, we needed advice and guidance on police procedures and we were lucky enough to have one of our beta readers turn out to be retired ex-Met police detective and fellow author, Mark Romain. He offered very kindly to read over our manuscript and give us pointers on how to make the police procedures more accurate and tone down some of the more clichéd things that writers sometimes include, like the fast car chases and the laser beams from gun sights.

ONE OF THE things that gave Mark a "shake my head and groan" moment when he read the manuscript for '**The Burying Place**' was the end scene where originally Rachel was holding up her hand to block the laser beam from a marksman outside the person she was about to arrest's house. Her exact line was (*originally*, we hasten to add) **"If I drop my hand it's all over. They'll shoot you."** Mark wrote on the manuscript, 'No. No this simply wouldn't happen.' We could almost feel the heavy sigh from him. Needless to say, with a little help on the rigmarole of hostage situations and the deployment of AFO teams from Mark, we rewrote the scene and the rest is history.

WE BLAME the fact that the night before we wrote that scene we'd watched '**Line of Duty**'. Our point is if you have a particular character in your book that someone you know or have access to could help you out with the finer points of their know-how in this field then don't be afraid to ask. Most of the time they will offer their insight and expertise for free, and a simple credit in the book is enough of a thank you, but occasionally you may be required to pay for their time and knowledge. After all, they need to make a living too, so it's only fair. Just make sure you check them out thoroughly before you part with your money, as the internet is rife with people who like nothing more than to separate people from their hard-earned cash. Look at their resume. What have they done before? Who else have they helped? Believe us, if they are worth their salt they will be glad to brag about their big gigs. If money is tight and you can't afford to get a researcher then it's time to hot-foot it down to your local library or archive centre. You might be lucky and catch the eye of the always-happy-to-assist librarian or resident historian who will be only too happy to point you in the right direction. While you're in the library why not check out the land registry and the census. This is a great way to look at old town plans and street layouts, which is especially useful if you are writing a novel about Victorian London. The first official Census was carried out in 1801 and detailed every household in the UK in terms of who lived where what their occupation was and their list of who was in their household. This is a great tool for finding names and specific jobs that were done in the year your novel is set.

IF YOU ARE WRITING a military novel then a key place to visit is a museum that has exhibitions centred around the specific war or era you are writing in. They will have glass cases full of war memorabilia, old uniforms, weapons and battle maps. Consider joining organisations such as English Heritage, National Trust and Historic Royal Palaces where, as a member, you can visit as many sites of historical significance and soak up their offerings which will help you when planning your masterpiece.

A LOT of authors travel to different places, even different countries, to immerse themselves in the vibe and culture of that place, which makes their novel so much richer from their own lived experience. Travel writers and television chefs do this all the time, why can't you? Take pictures, walk around, talk to the locals, eat the local cuisine, maybe even stay with a family who are born and bred there. You will gain a deeper, richer experience of the culture you are writing about if you have first-hand experience of it.

START TO MAKE notes about your new surroundings:

- Where are you staying?
- Is it an affluent city or a rural area?
- What politics are people governed by?
- What does the landscape look like?
- What are houses made out of?
- What colour are they?
- What's the weather like? What would the complete opposite to this weather look like and why? You can create tension in your writing by using what's called 'pathetic fallacy', This is where the mood of the story is shown by the weather. For example, if the weather is sunny then the scene is a happy, carefree one. If it then starts to thunder and lash it down then it's a clear sign that the lightness in the air is about to darken significantly. Think of the **Harry Potter** movies. How much does the atmosphere, temperature and weather change when the Dementors arrive on the scene? This is a perfect example of pathetic fallacy.
- What are the temperatures like in winter?
- How high did the temperatures get in summer?
- What type of car do the villagers drive?
- How much does it cost relative to the annual workers' wage?
- How much do things cost in shops?
- What shops tend to be in that particular town or city?
- What type of people live there?
- Do they work?
- What jobs do they have?
- What's the landscape like?
- Are the locals friendly, or are they cautious/suspicious?
- Are they happy and why are they this way?
- If they are suspicious, why?
- If always friendly, why?

- Do they live by the sea?
- Are they into surfing and fishing?
- And has everyone got a boat?
- What does a normal day look like in this location?
- What can you see?
- What can you hear? If they are by the sea can you hear the waves crashing, the seagulls squawking, or the wind howling?
- What can you smell? The salt in the air, doughnuts frying, or even petrol from the speedboats?

THE WHOLE POINT of immersing yourself in the local culture is to be able to paint the picture for the readers that you are seeing with your own eyes. Your novel will be saturated with gorgeous detail that the reader will thoroughly enjoy immersing themselves in too. Remember, show, don't tell.

HERE's a good idea for the movie buffs amongst us. A way to strengthen your knowledge and understanding of a particular location is to watch movies set in the same place and time as your novel. Here the location managers and top researchers have done all the heavy lifting for you and you can simply soak it all up for your masterpiece. On that note, we would strongly recommend you read as many books (fiction and non-fiction) in the genre and period your novel is set. Look closely as you read at how the author describes a person, their outfit or a location where the action takes place, but don't copy it.

Quote from co-author, Claire Hackney:

One of the main reasons I love reading C.J. Sansom's 'Shardlake Series' is because I am a massive Tudor fan and the richness of Sansom's descriptions mean I can almost smell the foul odours emitting from the London streets and can picture the clothes the characters wear and just how bushy their beard is from the subtle use of adjectives used by Sansom. I have never written a novel set in the Tudor times but if I did I would use Sansom's books as my muse.

THERE IS a Facebook group for everything under the sun these days. this is no bad thing for novel research. All you have to do to find experts in the area you need them is to type into the search bar what you are looking for and the appropriate group will be there for you to join. You can then ask your new friends questions about your chosen subject and receive answers that will help you no end.

So, now you are armed to the teeth with options of where to get your research for your novel, the next question is what do you do now? Where do you start? In your **'How to Write a Novel from Scratch'** workbook you will find several pages you can jot down your ideas on. There is 21 spaces so ample room for you to plan out some thorough and detailed research that will add a lovely richness and depth to your novel.

14

Locations

How to Write a Novel from Scratch - Workbook section 14

WHERE WOULD you like to set your novel? That's the big question, right? Will it be in this country, somewhere else, or even on another planet? Wherever it is it is crucial that you have a thorough, all-around understanding of what that **location** looks like, smells like and what the landscape and terrain is like.

THE FIRST CONSIDERATION should be which genre you are writing in, as this will be one of the deciding factors as to where your action mainly happens. The Wild West would be described in a completely different way to an English period drama set in Belgravia. Also, a science fiction story set three hundred years in the future will have a completely different aesthetic than a historical romance set three hundred years in the past.

ANOTHER THING TO remember when describing locations in your novel is that a historical novel will potentially take place in a place that does not exist anymore. A town that was part of the Wild West in the 1800s probably has shopping malls and houses now built upon it, or a medieval battlefield now might have a museum dedicated to it on site. Your novel will no doubt have more than one main location, it may have two or three, so for this reason in your **'How to Write a Novel from Scratch'** workbook there are three sections for your to plan out the details of your location research.

FIRSTLY, think about the type of people that live or work in your main location. We'll call that location 1. Are these humans? Aliens? Servants? The landed gentry? A London City banker? A bookshop owner? In the first space in your workbook write down everything that comes to mind about how these individuals look, dress, act, speak etc... This is very important as the narrative relies on you understanding if they speak with an accent, tone, don't speak at all, or even communicate in a completely different way - in an alien language, for example. Do these individuals have families? Do they have masters or slaves? Do they have work colleagues? How do they interact with them? Write down as clear a description as you can muster at this point. We have a long way to go yet, so don't worry if you can only get small details or singular adjectives out of your brain.

NEXT, think about the actual landscape of location 1. Is it an arid desert, all yellow sand and dry air, or is it the lush greenery of a Hawaiian island? Do your characters live on a 300-acre estate in the Cotswolds, or do they live in a tenement block in the slums of Glasgow? Picture this location you have chosen. Close your eyes and imagine the colours, shapes and sizes of each facet of the location you would like to be the setting of your main action.

IT IS STRONGLY RECOMMENDED you do at least a floor plan of the location that you intend to set your action in. This will ensure that every time you revisit it in your writing then everything that's in the room will be described as being in the same place. If the counter in your bookshop is directly opposite the front door and all the historical fiction books on the right of the room as you look at it from the counter then draw this on your floor plan. If bookshelves, doorways and counters suddenly change locations in the shop throughout the reading then your reader will feel disorientated as they read, causing them to lose faith in your ability as a storyteller. There are few things worse as a reader to all of a sudden be jarred from the page and think, "hang on, the wardrobe was by the window in the last chapter. Now it's by the door?" The same goes with what outfit your individuals wear. If they are described as having green fins and blue hair then sketch your character and colour it in, so you remember the intricate details every time you describe them, or they appear in a scene with another character. When we wrote the final part of 'The Shona Jackson Trilogy', **'The Beach House'**, we made sure to sketch out a floor plan of the house so we knew where the kitchen was, where the bedrooms were and where the driveway was, so we could accurately describe what features the room had and what you could see from the windows etc... We also drew out a town plan of the local village, so we knew where the Doctor's office was, where the bar and stores were and also where the road came into the town and where it exited from. This enabled us to be able to set the scene for the reader so they could picture the action as it happened accurately and immerse themselves in the story even more. Use the internet to search for house decor, cars, outfits and hairstyles common in your period, so you can draw upon these elements as extra colour and detail to your descriptions. Each layer of detail you add gives the reader another layer of enjoyment when reading.

ONCE YOU'VE GOT a good idea of your primary location in terms of its aesthetic, and you've done your floor and town plans, next think about the other individuals who live there. Are they friendly or hostile? How do you know? is it how they are dressed? How do they talk? How do they behave? Are they happy, sad, angry, resentful? Think about how they interact with the main character. Are they friendly or hostile? Why? Think about how you can show this in the descriptions of their location. If they are hostile to the main character is that because they live in a more deprived area? Are they hostile because they are jealous and think they were dealt the rough end of the deal? Alternatively, are they living at the mercy or grace of the lead character so therefore have to be grateful and therefore are respectful and happy? The colours they choose to decorate their dwelling with are key to whichever track you go down with this, as lighter, brighter colours imply happiness, whilst darker, more drab colours indicate poverty and deprivation.

FINALLY, for location 1, consider what a normal day looks like in this location. What time does the sun come up, if at all? What are the routines and habits that the individuals have in this location? Here is an excellent place to drop in sensory details.

WHAT CAN YOU SEE/HEAR/TOUCH/TASTE/SMELL in this location at certain times of the day or night?

ALL OF THESE little details add up massively to the 360-degree immersion of the reader in your imagined world.

SO NOW YOU have your first location all set out, it's time to think of your second and third location. Is it the opposite end of the land or is it just next door? Is it in the next town, next city, next planet to the first? Go through all the steps that you went through when planning location 1 and complete floor and town plans so you can picture the location. The clearer your vision the easier it will be for the reader to imagine it also.

THE LOCATION where your novel is set is crucial for the narrative to be accurately and purposefully communicated to the reader through your writing. You cannot expect the reader to believe your character is tragically deprived of food if their homeland is described with pastures green. Remember, you're not just creating a story with characters, you are creating a whole world within the pages of your masterpiece.

15

Plot Twist Ideas: Make Your Readers Go WOW!

How to Write a Novel from Scratch - Workbook section 15

LET'S BE HONEST HERE, who among us just adores a damn good **plot twist**? Just at the point where you think the whole shebang is going to be wrapped up neatly at the end, a massive whopper is dropped in for an extra punch. And what's the first thing we say? "I knew something was going to happen! I always thought they were a wrong'un, right from the start!"

WE LOVE IT. The satisfaction of knowing our suspicions about the cook were right. The lawyer in on the deal all along, or the bedraggled beggar turning out to be a secret millionaire, plot twists switch our thinking and shift our focus. They are a brilliant way also of ensuring our book is read at least twice, as the reader will re-read to see if they can pinpoint the individual breadcrumbs that they might have missed before they knew the twist. There are some books that we reread simply because we loved the twist so much, and many films.

. . .

So how do you plan the perfect plot twist? Writers tend to have their plot twist idea in their heads before they even finish planning the whole story. They know what surprise they want to pull on the reader and work their way back from that to leave enough breadcrumbs to hint but not give away their secret. As you write, you want to lull the reader into a false sense of security. You want to take them down a comfortable path, where everything they think they know is clear and straightforward, then boom, drop the bombshell on them that everything they have read so far has been completely wrong. Build their trust in the plot then ruin it by dropping them into a completely new set of circumstances. Shake up their understanding of the character's motivations and integrity, or conversely, give the villain redeeming features by making them the hero all along - or at least giving them a pure reason for why they cause such devastation in the narrative (although we're still not convinced Mr Darcy should have been forgiven by Elizabeth in Pride and Prejudice, even if it did all come good in the end)

Whatever you do, do not make your plot twist too obvious.
Then it isn't a twist at all if the reader gets the sense in advance of what is going to happen. It's ok to be sort of sure, or suspect that something is going to twist at the end, as this gives the reader reason to keep reading to see if they were right, but if you make it too easy then they will throw your book down on their heap of 'not worth my time' books with a disappointed sigh and eye roll. Believe us, if you ever - and we mean *ever* - use the 'it was all a dream' ending in your novel then you deserve never to sell another book again.

Remember, readers have heavily invested in your novel if they have made it right up to the last few pages. They are putty in your hand and as such deserve a good payoff for their labours. They will be highly annoyed if they get to the end of your novel and find a lazy, tacked-on ending, or half-hearted attempt at a twist that no one would have guessed and simply makes no sense at all given the character build up and events in the narrative. If you make your twist completely unbelievable then it will be exactly that. If there are not enough leads to your surprise ending then your reader will be left thinking, "huh? But how...what...I just don't buy that!" And this is the final nail in the coffin for selling your next book to them. As long as you have put in subtle steps in between the main story and the side plot you want to surprise them with at the end, which is exactly what will be looked for in the second read of your novel, your readers will believe and enjoy your plot twist.

Quote from co-author, Claire Hackney:

"It doesn't matter how often I watch 'The Others' or 'The Sixth Sense', I still enjoy the twist at the end. Mainly because the breadcrumbs have been dropped throughout the storyline, ones I only saw during my second and third viewing. Even to this day, I spot new things that surprise me. Although, controversially, I did see the twist ending of 'The Usual Suspects' coming a mile off - but that's just my suspicious mind. I never trust the quiet ones."

WE'VE COVERED what not to do, so let's move on to what you should do to create the perfect plot twist in your stories. Why not kill off a popular character early. It's horrible but *so* effective. The reader gasps when someone they have gotten to know in the first few chapters suddenly dies. But it can add to the hook of your story because now the reader is aware that literally, *anything could happen*. Nothing is off-limits if the most beloved character snuffs it in the first act. It makes the reader think, "what now? Where is this going?"

MAKE a character be related to another character, one they either knew or had never met before in their life until the very last act. Who here wasn't left open-mouthed the first time they heard the line, *"I am your father, Luke?"*

WHAT ABOUT JUST WHEN you get to the end of the narrative, when the villain is overpowered and the world saved, then another even bigger problem presents itself?

RIGHT AT THE end of **'Jurassic Park'**, when the raptor is about to strike a cowering and terrified Alan, Ellie, Lex and Tim, out of the shadows of the visitor centre emerges the massive T-Rex to grab a leaping velociraptor out of the air and chomp on it before flinging it into a skeleton of the T-Rex's ancestor. Great, we think. That solved that problem. But NOW what do the group do now they are faced with an even bigger predator in front of them. Luckily for our intrepid group, another raptor joins the fray and distracts the T-Rex long enough for the humans to do a runner to safety. This scene still puts the jaw on the floor every time we watch it, as all truly great final scenes do.

As WELL AS killing off a character early on in your story, what about bringing back a previously thought dead character right at the end, to shake up the narrative. This is especially effective when it is an animal that we thought we'd lost in the fight, but turns out to have been alive all along and saves the day in the end.

Quote from co-author, Claire Hackney:
It must be noted here that killing animals in your narrative is simply not acceptable. I'm still not over Artax in 'The Neverending Story'. No, really. I mean it.

ONE LAST IDEA for you to think about here in our search for the perfect plot twist is thus - what would happen if the main character, the one hell-bent on revenge - suddenly *freezes* at the point of action? What if they simply do not have the bottle to go through with the murder or assassination? What does the target have to say or do to make them reconsider, flinch or back out?

LET'S DIP into our **'How to Write a Novel from Scratch'** workbook now and start to jot down our ideas. Hopefully, your creative juices will be flowing and you have lots of ideas to choose from. So, pick your 3 best ideas and note them down in the spaces provided in the workbook. Note down if you think your reader would suspect this is going to happen eventually in the story and if so, how could you tweak it to send them the opposite way down the path of rumbling you.

THINK ABOUT if your plot twist idea would work given the parameters of your storyline, and if it would significantly change the dynamics to a point where the reader would think it unbelievable. If the latter is the case then again add in some more tweaks. It is better to tweak a plot twist than chuck it in regardless of if it will work or not just because you like it so much. Your readers will not thank you so on this one it is best to drop the ego.

NEXT, consider the 5 steps you will have to include before the big twist to ensure the plot twist "reveal" is as effective, punchy and believable as you intend it to be. Decide if you think the plot twist should happen in the first, second or third act for it to hit the hardest. Once you have made as many notes as you think necessary on your first plot twist idea, have a think about a couple of alternatives.

YOU WILL NOW HAVE three possible options, so you could either pick your favourite and most viable option or is there a way you could incorporate two or even all three of your twists strategically throughout the narrative. Remember though, don't shoehorn them in because you think the more the better. On this one, less is more. Especially if it is a whopper!

PLOT TWISTS in novels are most commonly found at the end of the book, but sometimes a massive twist can happen at the beginning. They have been known to be called 'wallop scenes' - which is what we are going to explore next.

16

The Wallop Scene - An Explanation

How to Write a Novel from Scratch - Workbook section 16

WHAT IS A **WALLOP SCENE**?

We made up this term.

It is a scene, most commonly found at the very beginning of your novel that throws your reader straight slap-bang into the thick of the action. There is no preamble, no getting to know the characters and no scene-setting and describing the weather. In the first few lines, something BIG will have happened, not just upsetting the applecart but completely obliterating it into a ball of fire. A wallop scene gets the reader stuck into the heart of the opening problem, and on some occasions kills off or significantly maims the main character, to literally wallop the reader and get them on their toes immediately. It's a sure-fire way of indicating to your reader that nothing is off-limits here, and no one is safe.

So, if we've decided that the reader is going to have a torrid time of it whilst reading your book, and is going to spend the next however many hours reading your story in a state of anxiety that any character they establish an affinity with is going to croak it in horrific circumstances, or have a terrible thing happen to them, why on earth would they read past the first chapter? What can be the point or benefit of a wallop scene?

WELL, it's quite simple. We love to be shocked. We enjoy being thrown into a pit of despair. It keeps us hooked on the next paragraph as we hope for a resolution, or to find out that our hard-done-to hero gains revenge for this despicable action. Wallop scenes take the reader's breath away, surprises them, shocks them but ultimately ensures that your book is stuck to their hands like glue. You know those "unputdownable" books you hear about? ? This is why. Dropping in a nice, juicy wallop scene in the opening is a sure-fire way to keep your readers reading.

So, how do you create a wallop scene?

Ok, let's think for a moment about the best opening scene we've ever read in a book, or even seen in a drama or film. What happened? Who was blown up? Who "ran out of time"? Right at the start of the 1998 film, **'Mrs Brown'**, starring Judi Dench, we have a scene involving a stormy night, and John Brown (played by the wonderful Billy Connolly) running desperately into a wooded area searching for something. Some of it is filmed in point of view mode as if we are looking through Brown's eyes. Then the camera spins around and we are staring down the barrel of Brown's pistol with an agitated Brown screaming "God save the queen", before firing the gun into thin air. It is the perfect "what on earth" scene. We are immediately hooked. We want to know what has drawn a man out of his bed in the dead of night to hunt in a forest for something only he can see. And what has the queen got to do with it? It is only towards the end of the film that we find out the relevance of this scene, but this wallop scene throws us straight into the thick of the action immediately and serves as the excitement in an otherwise slow-paced film.

HORROR MOVIES rely heavily on wallop scenes. Take a moment to consider the opening scene of the 1995 movie, **'Scream'**. For about ten minutes we are a spectator to the slow torture and demise of Drew Barrymore's character, Casey. With her, we are taken on a tour of her house as the slow realisation sinks in that the person she is on the phone with is taunting her and about to dispatch her most horrifically. The scene is brilliant and completely new in the fact that Barrymore was the most famous star in the movie but is killed off in the opening scene. Audiences at the time were completely shocked at the huge Hollywood star croaking it before they'd even got stuck into their popcorn, but there we are. The classic movie it became. And who amongst us will ever forget the opening scene in the 1977 film, **'Jaws'**? The character of Chrissie goes off for an unwise ocean swim after a few drinks and becomes the huge shark's first official movie meal. Amazing underwater camera work and the absolute terror of Chrissie's screams for help are juxtaposed with the eerie calm and silence moments later after the bite-and-drag under the water by our most loathed aquatic villain. This scene was particularly shocking and potent to audiences because the concept of the 'opening kill' trope hadn't yet been seen in movies. With Chrissie being the first character on screen, which is a role usually filled by the main protagonist of the story, who is then chewed up and swallowed, audiences were even more discombobulated by the rulebook being completely ripped up - leading them to feel a sense of unease that even more shocks were to come.

WALLOP SCENES ARE NOT ONLY FOUND in horror films. Yes, they are incredibly effective to set the reader/audience on edge early on (which is the horror film's main schtick) they are also becoming more and more common in other genres. The Pixar film, **'Finding Nemo'** is a classic example of how a wallop scene can hook in the audience. Unexpected in the way that it is rare to show peril in kids films on this scale. The opening scene involves the clownfish Marlin and his wife Coral talking about starting a family until a barracuda attack splits the family up in the most harrowing way. Little Nemo, not much more than an egg at this point, loses his mother and for this reason, Marlin is fiercely overprotective of Nemo. But Nemo grows to be an inquisitive fish, too much for his good and one day becomes separated from Marlin who then spends the rest of the film searching for him. The opening wallop scene is completely unexpected. What appears on the surface to be a fun little film about a silly fish getting lost and having lots of adventures starts with a highly emotional scene that still draws a tear from the eye to this day. But arguably, the opening wallop scene has made the film more memorable with it than it would have been without it. With it, the character arcs are so much more pronounced and the stakes are so much higher, as we truly understand on a much deeper level the importance of Marlin finding Nemo after watching what happened to his wife. Losing Nemo is simply not an option and an emotion that the audience well and truly buys into.

So, there we have it. Wallop scenes are crucially important in your novel planning if you want to hook your reader in from the start. You can still introduce your main character and describe the scenery and weather if you must. But it is done through the lens of dire peril, rather than a nice, comfy, sedate way of storytelling that doesn't challenge the reader's expectations in the slightest. Wallop scenes should grab the reader by the scruff of the neck and ensure that they are not released until the end of your book. Wallop scenes set the tone, dictate the play and put the wheels in motion for what is about to be the rollercoaster of a lifetime for the reader.

WE HEAR YOU. "That's great and all", you say. "But how do I write a wallop scene?" Let's continue…!

17

The Wallop Scene

How to Write a Novel from Scratch - Workbook section 17

To DEVISE the perfect **wallop scene** you must first decide on what your storyline is going to be and what would be the absolute worst thing that could happen. Remember the essence of what an effective wallop scene is - something that flips the action on its head and makes the reader feel completely shocked into asking, "what the hell just happened?" If they ask that you can guarantee they will turn the pages to find out. You are getting them addicted to your story from the get-go, drip-feeding them tiny morsels to keep them hanging on for the next one. Cruel it may sound, but no one reads books for a slow-paced, predictable and cosy story, with slow-paced, predictable characters. Even Miss Marple and Jessica Fletcher find themselves in perilous situations set up by wallop scenes plonked at the start of the action.

THERE ARE a couple of examples in your **'How to Write a Novel from Scratch'** workbook to get your juices flowing. Let's take a closer look at the first one.

**Somebody who is painfully shy at the very beginning of the book may be waiting to go out on stage. They get introduced, they walk out on stage, their big moment arrives. The character is about to open their mouth and... Nothing. Complete humiliation.
They then run off stage to boos and confusion.**

WITH THIS OPENING SCENE, the reader is involved straight away in a significant problem, and all the emotional turmoil that comes with it. Rather than spend the opening paragraph explaining that the character is shy and notoriously suffers from stage fright on big occasions we have gone straight down the 'let's humiliate the character instead' route - a classic example of show don't tell.

NOW LET's look at our second example from our workbook.

A bride is walking down the aisle looking radiant. Her eyes meet her husband-to-be's. they are about to say, "I do" when he says, "I don't love you anymore" and leaves the church where everybody is left open-mouthed.

THIS TYPE of opening is quite common in stories mainly because it is a brilliant wallop scene. It completely dumps the reader headfirst into a conflict, struggle or situation, and they cannot help but read on to find out how on earth the characters are going to cope with the turmoil created.

SO NOW IT's time to think of your novel and what could be a great wallop scene opening to it. In your workbook, there is space to write down three main ideas. Try to pick an idea for a different character each time, so then you can pick your most effective wallop scene. give each one a grade out of ten for its "wallop-ness" so you will be able to gauge which is the strongest one. That's the one to seriously consider opening your act one with.

ANOTHER TIP that is often used is to pick a scene that you KNOW will be in your story at some point that will blow your readers away and have THAT as your wallop scene.

AFTER THAT SCENE, you can write: **5 years earlier...**

START where it is logical to begin, but now your readers KNOW that something BIG is coming. They will be fascinated as to how whoever was involved will get out of that situation (if at all) or what happens next.

INSTANTLY HOOKED!

LET'S DRIFT back to our original story idea. Our wallop scene could be:

Little Sophie is running through a wood in the dead of night. She falls over a tree stump, looks up through tear-stained eyes and says in a shaky voice, "You. Why are you doing this to me?" End scene.

THAT WOULD PIQUE our interest definitely as readers.

18

The Basics

How to Write a Novel from Scratch - Workbook section 18

WE'RE GETTING CLOSER NOW to pulling together all the different strands of our novel plan, but before we begin to write our full outline we must consider **The Basics**. These basic elements of our story will help us compartmentalise our main thoughts so we can move forward towards our fuller, more detailed plan.

IN YOUR **'How to Write a Novel from Scratch'** workbook, you can now fill in the basics. Think about who your main character is. Briefly describe them, what colour hair and eyes they have, what clothes they wear, what their style is. Consider what their occupation is, so you can accurately describe what their workplace looks like and what their working day entails.

BRIEFLY DESCRIBE THEIR MAIN ALLY. This is a person, or animal, who is their most loyal companion and trusted friend. They could be a work colleague, old college roommate, best friend from childhood, army buddy, or they could even be a love interest who is battling the enemy alongside them. Describe their looks, their attitude and try and may them contrast to the main character where possible. You don't want your reader to get confused as to who is who.

THINK about what your main character's **external goal** is. This is the thing that needs saving, the problem that needs to be solved or the treasure that needs finding. Why is this external goal so important to your main character? What is their vested interest in this issue? Why does this need thing need saving, this problem needs solving or this treasure need finding? What are the stakes if this external goal isn't achieved? For the main character and for the world as we know it. These details are extremely important to have fleshed out later on, but for now, we can write a skeleton plan as to the external goal. This can help with the plot planning too.

WHO IS THE MAIN ANTAGONIST? This is the villain of the piece and the person/thing/entity that is stopping the main character from achieving their external goal. Who is this person/thing/entity? What do they look like? What tools/skills/weapons/powers do they have that will be the force for evil and that will stand in the way of the external goal being achieved? Make your antagonist as multi-faceted as possible, and remember that even the evilest of villains have some redeeming qualities. Not all villains are completely bad. Give them a few qualities that contrast with their evil nature. Is your villain nice to their family? Do they do charitable work? Do they do nice things before they kill their victims?

FINALLY, think about a rough ending for your novel. Will it all end happily? Will the hero get the girl? How will the antagonist be stopped? What is the fallout for all the characters?

. . .

ONCE YOU HAVE the basics down on paper you can then start on the basic plan, where you will flesh out your ideas into the specific acts each event will occur in. This is what we will go on to next.

19

The Basic Plan

How to Write a Novel from Scratch - Workbook section 19

THIS SECTION WILL GIVE you the tools to pad out your novel's **Basic Plan** further, by using the three-act structure model. In act 1 of your novel, you need to elaborate on what the main character's problem or issue is - their **external motivation**. We have already looked at this in the last chapter but now we are going to develop it further by adding to it the main character's *internal* motivation.

BY THIS WE mean the lesson the main character needs to learn throughout the narrative for their character arc to be completed. You also need to get to the heart of the character's 'why'. If the external goal is to save the planet from a renegade asteroid then what is the main character's internal goal? *Why* are they trying to save the planet? *Why* are they the ones to go up in a rocket and do the deed? Take our friend Harry Potter - can you tell we're massive fans? Harry's external goal is to defeat Lord Voldemort and save the wizarding world. His internal goal is that he wants to avenge his parents' death and whilst on his mission learns the value of true friendship and love.

. . .

IF YOU WORK out what the external and internal goal is for each of your characters you will understand them in greater depth and evolve them into fully rounded people who leap off the page into the reader's hearts and minds.

THINKING BACK to your character's main ally, try to describe them in greater detail using the external and internal goal model. Why is this person/animal/entity going out of their way to help the main character? What's in it for them? Why would they risk it all? For love? Loyalty? Payback for something? What does the ally stand to gain by the end of the story which will make their sacrifice worth it? Especially if it means they will have to die for their friend.

LASTLY, what is the plan? Using your workbook, you can map out the main character's basic problem.

ACT 1:
What is the **struggle** they face in act one? Try to sum it up in one or at most two clear sentences. Now we can move forward to act two.

ACT 2:
In act two we see the ally (in your **'How to Write a Novel from Scratch'** workbook the ally here is referred to as the 'guide') becoming more of a focus in our planning. The main character cannot complete their mission without the ally and the comfort or counsel they provide. But why? What dangers do they face together? Think about Samwise Gamgee, Merry and Pippin in **'The Lord Of The Rings'**. Frodo Baggins arguable cannot complete his mission without his trusty band of helpers, and given the trials and tribulations, they face together it is

crucial to the plot that this four stay together. But at what cost? Their lives are in danger constantly, all along the journey, but this is what makes the narrative so compelling. How can you include your ally (guide) in this act where they enhance the plot?

Act 3:

Finally, in act three we need to consider the implications of the plan succeeding or failing. If Harry Potter succeeds in defeating Lord Voldemort, how will it happen? What will it look like? Will he destroy him in an explosion? Will he kill him in hand-to-hand combat? Will he cast a spell that rids the world of his enemy for eternity? How will the final act play out? In your **'How to Write a Novel from Scratch'** workbook jot down some ideas, even if you are not sure which ones you want to go with right now. Get them out of your head and we can mould them later when you write up your complete plan.

CONVERSELY, what are the implications of the plan failing? If Harry doesn't defeat Voldemort, what are the repercussions? What happens to Harry's allies? What happens to the world they all live in? In a nutshell, what are the stakes? Flesh out your ideas and bounce them against the implications of the plan succeeding. This will give you options to intermingle the light and dark aspects of your basic plan. Let the plan succeed and fail at different points, as this will keep the reader on the edge of their seat.

FOR **'THE TALKING WALLS',** our original story idea, our three-act structure could go along the lines of this:

Act 1 – We discover DCI Tom Nichols' external goal and his internal motive for striving for this external goal.

Act 2 – Does Nichols need help from a killer in prison to help solve the case? Here we have a good option for a plot twist.

Act 3 – Here we discover what would happen if Nichols solves the case, or doesn't solve the case. We have the resolution to the main problem. We have character growth, we have character evolution.

So NOW WE have come to the point in our planning where it is time for you to think about writing the first line of your novel. Excited? You should be.

20

Your Opening Line

How to Write a Novel from Scratch - Workbook section 20

THE OPENING LINE of a novel is extremely important. It sets the tone straight away and dumps the reader slap-bang into your narrative world with a bump. So, what will *your* opening line be? What tone are you going to set from the get-go in your novel? This section of your **'How to Write a Novel from Scratch'** guide will help you to whittle down all of your ideas into one perfect opening line, one that is guaranteed to make an impact on the reader.

FIRST OF ALL, before you even start thinking of the actual words that are to go in your opening line, you must think about what your opening **scene** will be. Where does the story begin? Where are you going to drop the readers the second they read your opening line?

THINK ABOUT YOUR FIRST LOCATION/SETTING. Is the first character we meet on the beach? On a ship? In a garden? In a building about to explode? Are they running through a forest in the dead of night being chased by some kind of malevolent force? What is happening?

This will give you the overall pace of what your opening line should be. If your first character is running through a forest in the dead of night then there may not be a lot of dialogue, apart from puffs and pants and possibly screams for help, or a "leave me alone, please don't hurt me" vibe going on.

ADD in what kind of weather is occurring that same night. Is it lashing down with rain, is there a howling wind all around, making all the trees crackle and leaves whoosh? Flesh out what is happening in the first scene before you even think of the words in the opening line. Picture it in your mind. Jot down all the components of the scene using sensory detail. If you were standing in this forest right now what would you see, hear, touch, taste or smell in the environment all around you? The more details you can put in here, the clearer you will set the scene. Lastly, in this part, think about the time of day your opening scene is taking place. Is it first thing in the morning when your first character wakes up and realises their spouse is not next to them? Is it lunchtime when the office block your character works in has just received news that there is a bomb in the basement but no one is allowed to leave or else it will be detonated?

IN YOUR **'How to Write a Novel from Scratch'** workbook there are specially designated spaces in the **Your Opening Line** section, so make sure you jot down as many ideas as you can. Free write, don't edit at all. You want your ideas to be as wide-ranging as possible, then you will have lots of raw material to work with before you second guess yourself and discount a potentially brilliant idea.

FLICK back to **The Genre Bundle** section and pull out a few of the power words that you liked. Jot them down in your workbook. These last few sections of your novel planning guide are where we look back on what we have learned so far. These power words should be the ones that fit your idea of your opening scene.

Remember everything you are putting together should complement your rough novel plan, and enhance it into the best version of itself. In your workbook, you will see a long list of verbs that you can choose from to give you some exciting words to include in your opening line. When you have decided on your favourite ones, the ones that will oomph up your opening line write them in the spaces provided in the workbook. These verb choices should give you an idea of the emotion you want to convey in your opening scene.

IF YOU HAVE FOLLOWED this step-by-step plan to writing your opening line correctly, you should now have all the tools at your disposal to free write your opening paragraph. Remember, it is crucial not to edit at this point, just write. Write down the idea that comes to mind, even if you are just describing the action. the flowing prose will follow later. Just get that idea out of your head. Write what you can imagine the opening scene being, including the location, the weather and what the first character we meet in the opening is doing.

FOR AN EFFECTIVE OPENING LINE, free write an opening scene, then circle the second that there seems to be any kind of movement or action in the scene. Dialogue is a great way to open your scene as well. In the first book in our crime thriller series, **'The Burying Place'**, the opening line was, *"Don't fuck this up, Rachel."* Now, dropping the f-bomb in the opening line might be unconventional and a risky move given that not every reader will appreciate profanity in their books, it nonetheless grabbed their attention. Straight away the reader is thrust into the action and is in no doubt what the tone of the novel is going to be. This opening line also raises the question, 'fuck *what* up?' The reader needs to know what the stakes are, and what will be the consequences if Rachel does *fuck this up*. Has she fucked up before? If your opening line encourages the reader to ask these types of questions you know you have hooked them from the start as their mission, as we are naturally curious as humans, will be to keep reading the next line, then the next paragraph and then the next chapter to find out the answers. And that's what will make your novel a classic page-turner. Job done.

ONCE YOU HAVE free written your opening paragraph, go back over what you have written and circle the point where you feel the action has gotten going. Bingo. This is the content of what should be your opening line. Starting with dialogue is a great idea too.

ULTIMATELY, your opening line should be intriguing enough to make the reader ask questions, and be curious enough to read on further. Think of it as the "golden ten minutes" on Netflix. When you discover a new programme or film on Netflix you say to yourself, "I'll just give it ten minutes." After that time, if it's not grabbed you it gets turned off for something else that has caught your eye from the menu screen. Nowadays we consume books like we consume digital TV. Why do you think all books on Amazon now include a 'look inside' function, where you can read the opening ten per cent of the book so you can decide if it's worth your time and money. You just have to make sure your opening line is interesting and intriguing enough to hook in the reader, so much so that they read on.

FOR OUR ORIGINAL STORY, **'The Talking Walls,'** the opening line (which would be after the wallop scene we have come up with earlier in this guide) could be something like:

> **"It's a nasty one Tom, you up for it?" asked one of the forensics team after the body was discovered.**
>
> **"Jesus Christ, what a mess. Who did that to her?" DCI Nichols replied.**

WE COULD EVEN THEN GO BACK three months previously to see how Sophie got to this point of being dead in the woods. There are lots of possibilities, but each one would give the story a really strong opening.

IN YOUR WORKBOOK, write down what **your opening line** for your novel idea will be. Now we can move on to our almost final plan. It's all coming together now.

21

The Almost Final Plan

How to Write a Novel from Scratch - Workbook section 21

THIS PART of the guide is our penultimate stage of info-gathering from our rough novel idea before we completely plan out our novel from scratch, using all the great work we have done so far. **The Almost Final Plan** is exactly that. A chance to map out the novel plan's broadest features so we can drill down further into them for the complete plan, which is our last stage. So, grab your **'How to Write a Novel from Scratch'** and let's start filling in the first page of the 'almost final plan' section.

START BY WRITING in the gaps at the top of your page the title of your novel. You can flick back to the section in your workbook and this guide to refresh your memory on the title you chose, or if you've had a better idea since then jot that down in the title line. If you have considered putting your novel in a series, and this isn't the first workbook you've used then write what number your novel is in this series. Now think about the scene that has stayed in your mind since you first thought of it. Throughout this guide we have explored ideas of what makes a strong scene in the crime thriller genre, so flick back through your notes and read back over the best scenes you have plotted. There will no doubt be one in there that you just can't get out of your head. It is probably the scene that you have based the whole of your novel around, or at least one of the pivotal scenes in there. Write this scene down in as much detail as you can think of, then add why you think this scene is relevant. It could be because it gives a full back-story to the main character, or explains why they behave in the way they do. Or it could be the key love scene that the final ending hinges off. It might even be the opening wallop scene that you have been itching to put in a novel you write because it's so awesome. A lot of writers have their ending in mind before they even write a word. maybe this is your key scene? If so, write it in the gaps in your 'almost final plan' section. Decide where this key scene should go. Will it be in act one, as your opening scene or where the action develops, in act two where the is a complication or crisis the characters face, or will it be in act three where the stakes are at their highest and the climax is imminent? Follow these planning steps for the three best, most memorable scenes from your idea.

WE WILL NOW PLAN out how our main characters will behave in act 1. This is so we can start to plan out our character arcs. As we have already covered in this guide, the arc of each character is incredibly important, crucial even, to keep the reader fully invested in your story. The peaks and troughs of a character make them well-rounded and human, and the choices they make throughout the story take on new resonance as they change and develop as a person. Think of Ebenezer Scrooge in Charles Dickens' **'A Christmas Carol'.** Scrooge starts out as miserly and dour, but after being shown the error of his ways - and how he will inevitably end up if he continues down the path of selfishness and greed - he changes his ways and demeanour entirely and becomes the best version of himself imaginable. But all along the way, he is taught little lessons and each ghost, from Scrooge's past present and future teaches him something else to consider. His personality change doesn't happen straight away, his character arc maintains the interest of the reader by changing slowly throughout the novel.

IN ACT one we also need to come up with some inciting events to get the plot moving. An inciting event is something that kick-starts the action. An explosion; a declaration of love/hate or revenge that starts the character involved off on a path of chasing, destruction, revenge or redemption; or even a murder or death. These inciting events need to be big and bold, to ensure that the reader sits up and takes notice. Write down your favourite three ideas for act one and then pick your best one. This will more than likely be your opening act, your wallop scene.

WHAT NEEDS to happen in act one, to set the wheels in motion and get the action going? Write down in your workbook the key elements of act one that are crucial to the understanding of the reader as to what the stakes are in the story. Finally, write down what the key locations are in act one. These should all tie in with the inciting event and the character arcs. Now you have a comprehensive idea of what is going to happen in act one of your story, we can move on to the key points in act two.

THIS IS A REALLY good place to drop in some red herrings to the action. Red herrings are quite like plot twists in their design. They aim to redirect the reader's attention from the truth of the situation by leading them down the wrong narrative path. The reader is led to believe from the way the scene is written and the breadcrumbs of clues that are dropped that the murderer or perpetrator of the crime is somebody else, thus ensuring that the exposition at the end of the novel is as effective as possible. This also gives the reader the fun of trying to work out "whodunnit."

A GREAT WAY TO throw in a red herring is to have someone acting suspiciously at a funeral, let's say. Or someone who flashes angry looks at the mourners in the church, but hardly says a word at the wake. As we all know from our novel reading, the person who looks the most guilty and has the clearest motive is rarely the true perpetrator of the crime as this is way too obvious to the reader, but this character is usually the best choice of red herring as it focuses the reader's attention on them and diverts it from the other characters who could be contenders. Your red herring will probably be the person who appears at all the crime scenes, gets to know the investigating officers, gives endless statements to the police and is ever helpful. Anyone who watches crime dramas knows that this is a classic trope and will be seen through in an instant by any crime reader worth their salt, but that's ok. Your obvious red herring will get the reader thinking if it's *not* this person, then who could it be?

ALTERNATIVELY, you could make your red herring someone completely unexpected. Someone who isn't even introduced until act two, who has been on the police radar for a while but it's only now they have enough evidence to question them. Your lead up from act one into act two must aim to make the reader believe that this person is a bone fide contender for the perpetrator, as then when the *real* villain is exposed the reader will experience the wow moment that all writers strive to create in their writing. Agatha Christie was a master at this.

Quote from co-author, Claire Hackney:

"I've lost count of how many characters I have suspected whilst reading one of her novels. Everyone including the house cat has been a suspect in my mind at one point or another, and when I would find out "whodunnit" I have always been gobsmacked and satisfied when reading back over the clues in each chapter. Red herrings make the reader experience fun, challenging and frustrating in the best possible way."

WHEN YOU HAVE DECIDED on your red herring, jot down which characters will appear in act two and how they will behave. In your workbook, there are quite a few spaces for your choices as there will be more characters who appear at this stage in your novel, so therefore more options for red herrings. How they will behave in the act is very important to plan out as then the lead-up work to offering the reader them as a plausible option for the red herring will be believable.

WHAT NEEDS to happen in act two? Again, like in act one, think of what are the crucial events that are needed in this act to propel the reader through the central action of the story and headlong into the final act. These crucial events need to be linked and get progressively worse and worse until the hero is completely at a loss as to what to do to solve the main problem in the story. This is when they might need some help from an external source. What could that be? Once you have decided on this you can move forward to act three, where all the action plays out to the finale. Before we move on though, jot down your key locations in act two, so you can nudge the narrative onward to the last act.

Now IS the time to drop in your killer plot twist. This twist must turn the story completely on its head and make the reader go "wow!" Think of the best plot twists you've ever read in novels, or seen in movies or on TV. There's a reason why they are so memorable to you because they were so jaw-droppingly good. Think of **'The Others'**, **'The Sixth Sense'**, **'The Usual Suspects'**, and even the film **'Saw'** which has arguably the greatest plot twist we've seen for many a year. We won't give it away, but strongly recommend you go and take a look to see how the viewer is completely unaware throughout the film of a crucial element to the plot, then when it is revealed it is a truly shocking and stunning piece of filmmaking.

Quote from co-author, Vicky Jones:

"I was speechless for ages afterwards and immediately replayed the movie to see what I'd missed seeing what was right in front of my eyes the whole time."

THINK about your potential plot twist. What is the thing the reader would least expect to happen? Remember though, it must be plausible. There's nothing worse than a plot twist that is just a plot hole. A good, juicy twist must spin on its head everything the reader thought they knew about the character or situation, and become the complete opposite, or the worst possible alternative to the established set of circumstances the reader has been present in for the last several hours of reading. We have spent quite a while together in this guide thrashing out ideas and planning different plot lines that by now you should have a good idea of a couple of potential plot twists, so make sure now you commit them to paper and write them down. Out of your ideas, choose the one that makes you go, "wow, that would shock/surprise them!"

LET'S MOVE on finally to act three of our skeleton novel plan. Take your surviving characters to this point and move them forward into the final part of your action. How will each character behave here, given what they have been through in the previous two acts? This is where we drawback upon the character's arc. We now come down the last slope to see how everything that has happened to them has shaped and changed them as people. Consider also if you are going to introduce a brand new character in act three. It has been known to happen - think of King Richard the first in **'Robin Hood, Prince of Thieves'**. Sean Connery appeared for less than five minutes in the last reel of the movie, but is nonetheless extremely memorable in the role, not least for his inexplicable Scottish accent for a king who spent ninety per cent of his reign on shores other than England, and spoke in French most of the time. Throughout the movie, King Richard is referenced, but only makes an appearance in the third and final act. If you have a similar storyline, with someone who is mentioned throughout but hasn't appeared yet, drop them into the final act. Make sure you jot down in your workbook a clear and detailed description of how they would behave in this final act.

As YOU'VE DONE for act one and act two, write down what needs to happen in act three. This is where you aim to tie up all the loose ends in your story. Add in the locations that will be featured in your final act also. It goes without saying that your final act will include your ending, so it's time to start fleshing out how that ending will go, in general. Remember, this is the 'almost final plan' so we only need the skeleton of your idea at this point. Each section of this guide and the accompanying **'How to Write a Novel from Scratch'** workbook is to tease out of your brain the novel idea that has been rattling around in there in its basic form for as long as you can remember. The aim is to get it out of your head and down on paper. The ending is the bit the reader has been waiting for, and no doubt the part you have been itching to write. We'd go as far as to say it was probably the first thing you thought of before you even thought of how to connect the ending to a story. So, here we are. The final showdown with the protagonist and antagonist facing off against each other in a do-or-die situation. It is the part the readers have been looking forward to so you must give them something worth their hours of reading up to this point.

IN YOUR WORKBOOK, you have three spaces. Think of three ways your story could end. Is everything going to be tied up nice and neatly, with all characters apart from the villain having a happy ending? Are you going to kill off a beloved character? Are you setting up a sequel hence leaving everything teetering on a cliff-hanger? Whatever your decision is, it must satisfy the reader and ensure their labours haven't been wasted all these hours for a piffling, weak, pointless "huh?" type of ending. all loose ends must be tied up, even if you are planning on ending on a cliff-hanger. In this case, leave one significant strand hanging so it will whet the reader's appetite to return to the table once your next instalment of the series is released. When you have chosen your three best potential endings it is now time to pick your best, most effective and powerful ending. It might not be the one you originally planned before we started on this journey together, but that's fine. It's all part of the evolution process when you are planning your novel. You end up moving on from your original ideas when you put more thought into them and see that maybe something else would work better. This doesn't mean that your original ending is no good at all though, it might crop up again in a different novel you plan, where it fits better with the plot, so don't get rid of any notes you've made on this previously. Save them for the next time.

So, there we have it. Your **Almost Final Plan** for your novel is down on paper. Take a moment to congratulate yourself on all your hard work so far. You now have a fully thought-out skeleton of your plan. It is now time to put everything we have learned in this guide together one last time in the complete plan for writing your book.

22

The Complete Plan For Writing Your Book

How to Write a Novel from Scratch - Workbook section 22

HERE WE ARE. The last stage of our epic journey together from blank page to complete first draft of your novel. So far, we have covered:

YOUR WHY - WHY do you want to write a book at all?

THE FOUNDATIONS OF A GOOD BOOK - how to understand and employ the basics of writing a book.

THE FICTION SQUARE - how to come up with ideas for your novel.

YOUR TITLE - how to create the perfect title for your novel.

. . .

GENRE BUNDLE: Crime - how to incorporate the main elements in the crime genre into your novel.

CRIME BOOKS: Do's and Don'ts - how to avoid the clichés that come with crime writing.

ENDINGS - how to write the perfect ending for your novel.

CHARACTERS - how many characters you will need, their traits, quirks, descriptions, and arcs.

RESEARCH - how to research your novel.

LOCATIONS - how to choose the perfect locations for your novel.

PLOT TWIST IDEAS - how to give your novel a bit of spice with the perfect plot twist.

THE WALLOP SCENE - how to make your readers sit up and pay attention from the very first sentence.

THE BASICS - how to outline your plan.

YOUR OPENING LINE - how to come up with the killer opening to your novel.

THE 'ALMOST FINAL' PLAN - how to include the main elements of each scene in your novel.

LASTLY, we come to **The Complete Plan for Writing Your Book**. This is where you will put in a comprehensive plan all of the great work you have done whilst following this guide so you will be able to *see* your novel from start to finish. This is the part where it gets super exciting. When all your ideas come together on the page. Where you see your novel all ready to be written.

THE COMPLETE PLAN template in your **'How to Write a Novel from Scratch'** workbook includes all of the elements you will need to include in your novel on an easy to fill in template. Simply fill in the blanks and your novel will appear before your eyes.

So, without further ado, let's start filling in those blanks.

IN THE COMPLETE PLAN, we will break down the full novel idea into the traditional three-act structure. This will give us a nice balance to the flow of the novel. Firstly we will outline the events in act one.

YOU NEED to make your final decision on your opening line. Flick back to your notes in your workbook if you have forgotten, then go right ahead and write it in the space provided in your complete plan section. Remember, a great opening line must grab the reader's attention instantly. Some readers like a punchy expletive-laden line, but some don't, so be mindful of your potential audience. Personally speaking though, we don't mind the f-bomb being dropped in on the first line. When we see this in an opening line or paragraph we instantly think that this is a bold, confident crime/psychological author who is and ready to take us on a no-holds-barred ride through some dark themes and plot lines. We're not there for the picnic, we're there for the murders and conspiracies, so a bit of cursing just adds to the devil-may-care attitude of the author in the narrative. But, be mindful that there are some less battle-hardened readers out there than us who prefer their ride a little smoother and not as spicy.

Y‍OUR WALLOP SCENE must also pack a punch. What is the event that will kick your rollercoaster novel off? Will it be a murder/death? A crash? A funeral? How can you want to introduce your action and main character in the most memorable, dramatic way? Remember to 'show, not tell' the setting. Describe the location using the five senses that the main character is experiencing, as this will immerse the reader in the environment straight away.

ONCE YOU ARE past your opening line and wallop scene, give the reader a 'first look' at your protagonist's normal life. What are they doing? What is their a-typical behaviour? So, if you have a main character who is very ordered and neat, you could have them in their office placing books on their shelves in spine-coloured order, or alphabetical order. Make them quite methodical about it. Or are they super clean and well-dressed? Include a scene where they line up their clothes the night before work and layout their toiletries ready for their morning shower. Or are they the total opposite? Are they chaotic, messy and badly behaved? These little details help the reader build a picture of the protagonist from the get-go, which will help them go with you as the protagonist's character arc starts to emerge later in the story. Add in a flaw or two with your perfectly ordered and behaved protagonist. Are they really bad at socialising so they leave their phone on silent, or turn down dinner plans with friends? Likewise, add in a good trait or two to your chaotic, messy, badly behaved protagonist. Make them sweet, funny and a great, albeit absent father. Make their daughter love them even if they are hardly in their life because of a bad marriage break up. Go back to your character notes and use the ones which best represent your character at the beginning of their journey through the events in the story.

THINK about what your main character wants from their life and why? Are they near their retirement date and just want to see out this last case before sailing off on the yacht they bought twenty years ago and have only just finished refurbishing or paying off? You need to have something at stake here, otherwise, the main character's raison d'être is simply not there. What are their motivation and goals? Is this a current case with a serial killer who has struck again? Has this killer been dormant for years and now there is a new murder that has the same modus operandi as the historical killings? Can your main character face going through all of this again, when last time they almost cracked under the pressure? All of these factors need to be established early on in the narrative for the character arcs to develop into acts two and three. When the events of the wallop scene are made apparent to the protagonist, what is their reaction? Are they at home and they get the phone call to come into the station? Do they see a news report? How does this affect their behaviour at home? What do they see/hear/feel? The reader needs to be able to picture the reactions of all involved. Show, don't tell. Do not under any circumstances use phrases like,

"This made John very angry when he saw the news report of the plane crash."

DESCRIBE JOHN'S physical reaction to this news.

"John swept his arm across his perfectly ordered coffee table, sending his files and papers skewing across the mahogany. With his fists clenched and eyes darting around the room, his pulse raced as he realised there was

nothing he could do. The flames licked higher around the building that was front and centre on his TV screen."

CAN YOU SEE THE DIFFERENCE? The reader still gets a clear impression that John is angry, but you can *show* anger must more descriptively than just using the word *angry* in your writing. Describe what they are doing when they hear the news. What is their next move? Do they call anyone? Do they race out of the door to get to the scene? Build up the tension with action at this point. When your protagonist gets to the scene, what do they do? Who is the first person they look for and why?

WHAT OTHER FLAWS appear in your protagonist's personality? While racing through the traffic to the scene of devastation they have heard about, are they short-tempered in the traffic? Are they rude and aggressive to the windscreen cleaner who jumps out at them at the stop sign and demands a tip? How are these flaws affecting your character's day-to-day? Does their attitude affect anyone else (other than the poor windshield cleaner!)? Think about all the strands of possible storylines here. Where are the side stories? What opportunities does this give you to expand on the narrative and drop some breadcrumbs in for later?

NOW WE COME to the inciting event. This is different to the original wallop scene, which purely serves as the scene that makes the reader sit up and pay attention. The inciting event further develops this wallop scene. For example, in your wallop scene at the beginning we had the "sit up and notice" introduction to the main threat in the storyline. The asteroid hurtling through space; the first murder by our serial killer; the first bomb that went off. The inciting event is the event that gets the protagonist involved. What could happen that involves them personally? Has a second bomb gone off in their police department? Has their significant other been kidnapped or is trapped in that building which means the protagonist now has to save the day? What event can you involve here is enough to incite the protagonist into action? This must also match what you envisage being an organic forward thrust of their character. If their estranged partner who they hate with a passion has been kidnapped or is trapped in a building then there is very little if any believability in the protagonist risking their lives to save them. Conversely, if the person trapped is the spouse or partner of the protagonist that they were calling on the way to work to make romantic anniversary dinner plans with then it makes sense that them being held hostage or being trapped somewhere would light a fire in the protagonist to make them want to save them - preferably in time for their reservation.

WHAT CONVERSATIONS ARE BEING HAD between the characters? How would they react to this inciting event? When the first plane hit the north tower of the World Trade Centre in New York on September 11th, 2001 there was mass panic and anguish at this seemingly terrible accident that had befallen the pilot, passengers and occupants of the plane and tower. Contrast that reaction to when the second plane smashed into the south tower. Panic and anguish escalated into hysteria and finally complete disbelief at what had happened - and why.

Quote from co-author, Claire Hackney:

"Every time I watch footage of the second plane hitting the south tower I am met with the same feeling - complete horror and head-shaking disbelief. Each time I see the footage it feels like the first time. I am convinced each time there will be a different outcome. This can't be happening. That didn't just happen, did it? I watch the different angles and each time I'm convinced the plane will just fly right by the tower. But when I see it hit I still can't believe it. The news reporters try their best to remain composed but several can be heard on live reporting feed howling and shrieking with utter horror. The anchorman or woman pressing their finger to their ear and pausing in disbelief and shock at what they were hearing over the live feed."

Now, we are not comparing the events of 9/11 with a plotline to your novel at all - the magnitudes are incomparable. Our point here is that whatever your inciting event is and whatever the planned fallout of it is, make sure the reactions match the scope. Make sure the behaviours of the characters match the gravity of the situation. Don't over or underplay it. Melodrama has its place in fiction, but too much and your reader will be distracted by this and not the subtlety of the characterisations you are building.

AT THIS POINT, it is important to consider the protagonist's internal and external goals. What are they? Why these specific goals? For example, if your protagonist arrives at work to find out their family is trapped in a building about to be blown to smithereens if somebody doesn't intervene, that there is the external goal. To save their family. But what is the internal goal? Why does the protagonist feel in their soul that there is a need to do this? Are they doing it out of love? Is it for some kind of redemption? This internal goal propels the protagonist forward to achieve their external goal. The way you as the writer create the peaks and troughs of the protagonist's character arc will be crucial at this point to engage the reader and get them to root for your character and follow their progress with bated breath.

THINK BACK NOW to your character flaws. What if the family are being held hostage at the top of the building and the protagonist is deathly afraid of heights or even lifts? What if Bruce Willis in **'Die Hard'** was claustrophobic? Those air vents would have been a nightmare, but would have added an extra edge to the scenes where he finds out *"how a TV dinner feels."* An important consideration further on in the plot is whether or not the antagonist knows about this flaw in the protagonist's character and how the antagonist will exploit it for their gain. But we will come on to this more later.

It is about now that the first act of your novel's 3-act structure will come to an end. The scene has been set. The protagonist is introduced and the main threat of the piece is made apparent. The fatal flaws of the protagonist have been exposed, their Achilles heel uncovered, and we now see what is at stake. It is the perfect time to set up your act one cliffhanger. Normally, you see some kind of tragic event, the external goal thwarted in some way, leaving the characters to stare helplessly at a screen that has abruptly gone blank and all contact with the hostages has been lost. Picture the scene you are going to write to end the first act. It must pull at the heartstrings or get the adrenaline going. Use your sensory details to immerse the reader in the action. The words you choose can leave the reader thinking, "What the hell happens now?" All seems to be lost. They understand from the number of pages they have left to read that it's not the end of the book, so there must be another solution, option or plan from the protagonist and their allies presented to the reader in compensation for their shredded nerves from act 1. This is where the story's master plan is formulated. The protagonist will think up some kind of idea that will get the group inside the building and aim to free the hostages, kill the baddies and save the day. This is the scene that will kick off act two.

Revisit briefly the 'thwart to the goal' you ended act 1 on. What went wrong? The main characters involved will probably have some kind of debrief to thrash out where the blame lies. No doubt the protagonist will be frantic with worry and anger, knowing their family is in even more peril than they were before. Here we should get to know the protagonist more from an internal perspective. One of their allies should sit with them and find out more about why they are so keen to save their family. There should be a lull in the action where the dialogue comes into its own. This is when the real character building can be done and you can concentrate on building up the affinity between the reader and the characters. The reader needs to work out why they should care about this situation. It must speak somehow to them directly, so you as the writer must make the peril seem relatable. Even if you don't have a daughter, son or even parents, the notion of someone you love and care about deeply being in danger resonates on a common level. The devil is in the detail, so don't think the reader won't care because they aren't married or have kids. You can make a reader feel anxious and keen for a positive outcome by the power and depth of your language and scene-setting.

JUST AS WE are getting to know the protagonist on a deeper level and having a break from the chaos, we are going to throw in a whopper of a plot twist. Everyone loves a good "hang on a minute... what?" moment. What could yours be? What would fit this moment in your story? Make it big! Make it unpredictable. Does the protagonist know the villain? Have they crossed paths already at some point in the day? Is the villain the nice old guy the protagonist gave his seat up for on the subway? The fun part of writing a plot twist is how you expose it in the narrative. How will you describe the character's reactions to the plot twist? What could be the absolute worst thing to happen at this point in the story? What if the protagonist sees a picture of the villain on the news and recognises them as the windshield cleaner he yelled at on his way into work on a previous day? What if he realises at this point he could have stopped the villain if only he'd known what was going to happen? Linger on that moment when the grim realisation sinks in with the protagonist. You want to be able to almost hear the reader groan with anguish, just like the character. This leads us nicely onto our next section of the complete plan and that is the protagonist's new drive for their goal.

THINK about what the plot twist did for the narrative and what the stakes are now. Now would be a good time to introduce a brand new character into the mix. Who will this be? It should be an ally to the protagonist here, to have the best effect on the character growth. The plot twist has left the protagonist feeling vulnerable, weak even. the twist exposed their fragility as they didn't see it coming. They made a mistake. Took their eye off the ball maybe? So the new character ally must replenish their ego in some way and help to drive the narrative forward. Maybe they are the leader of the task force who has been drafted to storm the building? The protagonist must shake the fog from their head and focus. The ally is there now in the narrative to bring them around and brief them on what is going to happen. Could you even set up a smidgen of a love interest here? Just a thought to add another dimension here. It's your novel remember, you can do what you like as your fingers grace the keys on your computer.

NOW WE HAVE ADDED a plot twist and a new character, let's mix it up a bit more now by adding in a red herring. Red herrings as we have already looked at are elements in the story that lead us down the wrong path. People who we thought we knew, things we thought were real, even villains that weren't the true enemy. What could you sprinkle in here to get the reader properly engrossed? Our advice would be to have a couple to choose from, as readers of crime novels tend to be exceptionally shrewd at spotting the perceived culprit very early on in the narrative. That's fine. let them think they know whodunnit. But send them down the garden path by making the suspect potentially anyone in the story by giving each character a few shifty lines, or a bit of a dubious past. You want the reader to be changing their mind every time another character looks a bit dodgy. Here you have to be very careful though. You must plan this stage very well, as there is nothing worse as a reader when a writer loses track of the reasons why the reader would suspect that particular character. You as the writer must breadcrumb the clues in very carefully, so as not to be too heavy-handed that it gives off a clear red flag, and well enough that by the end the reader will be kicking themselves that they missed all the signs that Johnny was a wrong'un.

REVISIT the new plan once you have introduced the new ally and dropped in the red herring. How is this plan going? More than likely it is going wrong, as it is still only act two of your novel so the solution hasn't been worked out yet. Think about what conversations are taking place between your characters. Has your new character (the ally) been properly fleshed out in the novel? Can the reader formulate a clear picture of them in their head? If you feel you have overlooked this part, now is the time to add in more details about them. What traits are being shown by this new ally? How do they complement or jar with the protagonist? This is where you can start to deep dive into your character arcs. Cement the bond between the protagonist and the ally with tales from their background maybe? We are leading up to the first main attack by the antagonist so there has to be some kind of relationship gel building up between the two heroes.

MOVING SWIFTLY on to the antagonist's attack. What can that be? Is there a big explosion or does a body suddenly fly through the air and land on the protagonist's car? Has the first hostage been dispatched in the most traumatic way as to make the protagonist angry and fired up to take on the antagonist before the next unfortunate person is killed? You have a lot of options here, but whatever you decide you need to make it big enough to make not only the protagonist angry but also the reader, as this will propel the narrative forward and keep your reader hooked. We love it when a character vows revenge, especially when the writer makes the villain so hateful. Consider what the antagonist is thinking and feeling. This is a great time to give the antagonist a little bit of light and shade. Remember what we said earlier about villains - they are not completely irredeemable. They always have an Achilles heel. It is hard to find a villain that has no positive qualities. They tend to be incredible leaders and orators. Adolf Hitler, evil though he was, was an inspirational leader for most of the German people. He inspired the military to fight for the Reich, and a new generation of young people, the Hitler Youth, hung on his every word at the Nuremberg rallies. He inspired an entire generation of people to fight and die for the Nazi flag. Your villain must have something that sets him apart from complete evil. What are they committing these horrific acts for? What is their raison d'être? Write in a few scenes involving the antagonist if they are human in your story, possibly an anecdote about their back story.

WE ARE COMING to the mid part of act two now, so the clock ticking down to disaster, whether literal or metaphorical, should be ticking now. What are the stakes now? Have they changed, improved or got worse? What is the urgency? What happens if the clock ticks to zero? Will the protagonist watch on helplessly as the building his family are in exploded into smithereens? If this is the epic finale option that will hopefully be avoided at the last moment, then this imminent threat is what will ramp up the urgency of the resolution and add in even more tension to the narrative. Of course, the final resolution is not going to happen until the end of act three so we need to give the protagonist a small victory over the antagonist. We need at this point in the narrative a punch-the-air moment to keep the reader cheering for your hero. What can that mini victory be? Maybe the protagonist succeeds by infiltrating the main gang and taking out their communications system, leaving the money transfer they have asked for in peril. It needs to be a victory that the antagonist doesn't expressly know about has been caused by the protagonist, as if the baddie is holding hostages then they may start shooting in revenge. We don't want this as the reader will just think, "what a stupid thing to do" and lose faith in your hero. It has to be subtle. Smart. Something that drives the narrative forward but does not put the kibosh on the protagonist's master plan.

TIME FOR ANOTHER PLOT TWIST. Just to make the reader's experience just that little bit more uncomfortably wonderful, drop in a "what's the worst thing that could happen here" event. Give the antagonist another opportunity to strike. The bad guys are closing in on their mission. Time is ticking down even more. Don't forget to keep using your sensory details. Describing the smell of the smoke from a recently fired gun, the sound of the fuse in a stick of dynamite coming to its end, the sight of a fireball ripping through the upper floor of the building can have a massive effect on the reader, much more so than if you simply wrote, "the building blew up with a huge bang". What happens now? There is usually a frantic and emotional scene where the protagonist has to either calm someone down or be calmed. There will be a new plan formulated and they will go again at the villain. There will be a "what should we do" conversation happening between the characters who are working with the protagonist. At this point, you could bring in the cavalry. Another team could show up with more resources t put the villain out of action for good. Use this section in your **'How to Write a Novel from Scratch'** workbook to set out what conversations will happen here.

THE FIRST "BATTLE SCENE" should be present here. Whatever genre of novel you are writing, the "battle" can be physical or cerebral, but there should be a nice, juicy interaction between the protagonist and antagonist here. It is also a great opportunity to start killing off a couple of characters, maybe even for extra emotional effect, you could bump off a beloved character. This is a great way of changing the dynamic between the hero's team and the villain's cronies. Lay on thick the emotional impact of this death. It should be a deftly handled scene, using strong character reactions so for this part ensure you have built your main characters well so their reactions to this death are perceived as authentic by the reader. If you have two characters who are bland and hardly know each other it makes no sense whatsoever if one gets killed and the other wails in anguish when they find the body unless you have subtly built a reason for this through your character descriptions and backgrounds.

THE BATTLE HAS GONE WRONG. A beloved character has sacrificed themselves for the greater good and the antagonist has not been defeated. What happens now? What is the fallout from this? Was the death the protagonist's fault? This could give you a really interesting character arc moment. How does this affect the protagonist? Think about whether you want your reader to feel sorry for the protagonist because of this mistake that had tragic consequences, or does your protagonist now need to win back the respect and loyalty of the reader by how they bounce back and redeem themselves? This decision will give your protagonist's character arc a really interesting dynamic. This is also a great place to slot in an impact scene. If the person who has died was a close colleague, have the protagonist take a moment to themselves away from the rest of the group for a scream into silence or a cry into the dark, whilst holding a piece of the deceased person's clothing for example. This impact scene will show the character's humanity and peek behind the curtain of their tough exterior. Consider what inner demons the protagonist will have to face and/or fight off now, and what the effect of their inner turmoil will have on the others in their team. Think about how the protagonist's inner turmoil will become their external motivation to take on the villain and defeat them for good, and in turn avenge the death of their friend and colleague. What traits is the protagonist showing here? Think back to the original character traits they had and what kind of person they were. The events in act two should have changed them and addressed or exacerbated their flaws. The only thing that can save the day now is the protagonist's reaction to the devastating events of act two. This leads us nicely on to the final act - act three.

THE FINAL SHOWDOWN is now ready to write. The stakes are high, the desire for revenge palpable and the protagonist and their team baying for the antagonist's blood. What happens now? You want the final act to be the culmination of all the plot lines and character arcs coming together, with the flaws resolved or capitalised on, so that the hero wins the day and the villain is defeated. So how will this play out? Most writers have a general idea of how their ending is going to go, some even have a great idea for an ending and write the rest of the book around it, almost working backwards through the narrative. If this is you then great, your ending should be relatively easy to write. There are some main things to remember though. You must resolve all of the threads that you have woven throughout your plot so that there are no loose ends. Believe us, the reader will notice them and there is nothing more annoying as a reader to ponder on the book just read thinking, "hang on, we never found out what happened to Johnny after he left to go and get help." Of course, you want the reader to think about your book long after they have read the last page and closed the cover, but you want it to be for the right reasons. You want them to marvel over your storytelling, not criticise you for your plotting. Write down all of your plot lines and make a conscious effort to tie all of them up in the final act. Give characters the send-off they deserve. Remember the little details you have breadcrumbed throughout the narrative. Your reader will get a kick out of the smallest details you have remembered and find your resolution highly satisfying, as to them it will feel like you have truly considered their reader enjoyment. No one likes a sloppy, forgetful writer.

WHAT HAVE your characters learned about their flaws? Has your hero conquered their fear of heights and now can abseil a building to get into the 156th floor to save the day? What is the plan to overcome the villain? How will the main problem of the story get fixed? Time to think big though, your readers don't want a gentle descent to earth, they want a few false endings, a lot of action and a boatload of peril and uncertainty. Who will survive? Make every character fair game. Make it unpredictable and above all make it make perfect sense for all characters and plot lines to end this way.

How's that ticking clock going? How much time has the protagonist got to save the day? This countdown will raise the stakes significantly, as it forces the characters to think and act quickly, and mistakes may be made. What conversations are taking place between the main players in the plan-making? Are they agreeing or disagreeing? This adds another layer of peril, as the characters must trust each other if they are going to be a united force against evil. When you write these final scenes remember to show and not tell. The reader wants to feel the stress and rush of time ticking down. Write your characters wiping their brow, biting their lips and getting short-tempered with each other as the countdown clock ticks. Avoid writing, **"They were all getting stressed because they were**

running out of time." This is way too easy to convey emotion to the reader. They want more. They deserve more. Give them more.

So, here we go. The final plan to overcome the villain is being written. What is the plan? Here we need pace in your writing. Short sentences and paragraphs give the sense of 'there is no time to lose, we need to get this done'. Long, flowing lines of prose allow the reader to relax and bathe in the warm waters of your descriptions. Rip them from their comfy seats. Blow something up, kill someone off. Jolt, even fling, the reader out of their armchairs by unleashing chaos and hell in your narrative. What time is on the clock? Has it ticked to zero yet? As it gets closer and closer crank up the tension. Have more noise, have some shouting, have some fistfights, or even some running. the adrenaline needs to be pumping through the veins of the protagonist and also the reader. They cannot and should not be able to put your book down at this point. All appointments must be cancelled, they must fear being late for work, or not be able to switch the bedroom lamp off because they are completely engrossed in your action. Pace, pace, pace is key here. Quick chapters, short paragraphs and no long monologues. There is no time. The world is at stake.

LET's do the unthinkable here and drop in a massive plot twist. And when we say massive, we mean gargantuan. The ally is the villain all along. They have been using the protagonist to get closer to the target/money/asset to take it for themselves, but couldn't do it without the knowledge of the hero. A 'double-crosser' may be a bit of a cliché but if you think about it, most if not all character tropes have already been done in the past. It all comes down to the *way* your characters and storylines are described. No one's ever done it like you before, so unless you carbon copy a plot/narrative/character from another book/screenplay then you are creating something unique in your novel here.

. . .

So, now we have two villains to defeat. We would suggest dispatching the original villain first, as this is the lesser of the payoffs. The original villain was the focus of the first two acts of the novel, but we now have a much worse villain. One who has betrayed the trust of our hero so, therefore, committed a more heinous crime in the moralistic stakes. Get rid of the original villain quite simply, but ensure you plan and focus on the new villain, the ally who has double-crossed our hero. What a snake! This person needs an ending that befits the level of betrayal they have caused. This will be the focus of the final battle in the novel.

IN YOUR FINAL BATTLE SCENES, remember the three 'c's here. Carnage, casualties, conclusion. Think of how you want your battle to play out. Is it hand-to-hand combat? A shootout? A more suspenseful cerebral battle of minds? This last option is admittedly less action-driven but it nonetheless can be incredibly enjoyable for the reader, especially if they are into such activities as chess or a game of wits that they can be involved in as the protagonist follows the clues and works out the mystery. The character arcs are now panning out to reveal what the new version of the character is. Their original flaws are now their strengths. They are changed. Improved. Better people for their experiences throughout your novel. At the end of the final battle make sure you reference how the characters have changed and complete your character arcs for them.

NOW THE LAST consideration is whether you want to tie up every single loose end in a nice bow or end your story on a cliffhanger. This is where you take one single strand of your narrative and leave it open-ended. Is the reader categorically sure the villain is dead or has been arrested? This is your call, but if you are writing a series you will need to give the reader some reason why they should buy your next book. Always leave them wanting more, that's our advice.

23

Conclusion

THERE WE HAVE IT. You have written **'The End'** in your novel. Yes, you have, even though you feel it's pretty cheesy, you have written it. But so you should. You have come a massively long way from the very start when your ideas were just randomly flying around your head with nothing to stick them together. You put these ideas into your **Fiction Square**, then plotted out your **Character Arcs** and planned your **Opening Lines** and your **Endings**. You have completed your Research and sketched out your **Complete Plan**.

CONGRATULATIONS. You have completed your full plan for writing your novel. Your **'How to Write a Novel from Scratch'** workbook is now full to the brim with your ideas, but not only that, your ideas are now in a nice, clear and logical format so you can simply start to write your novel. you don't even have to think of your first line. You have that. You have done all the hard work, so now all you need to do is start a new Word document and start typing up your notes.

. . .

ONE LAST WORD ON THIS. Never feel you are completely restricted to every element of your plan. As we discussed earlier, a great writer is neither a 'plotter' nor a 'pantser.' A great writer is a combination of both of these types of writer. The ability to plan a solid novel outline, but the freedom and confidence to come off that plan if a better idea emerges along the way is the perfect mix of both planning styles.

ABOVE ALL, be you. Your readers want to hear your voice in your writing. Write how comes naturally to you. What you have with your **'How to Write a Novel from Scratch'** workbook is all of the elements you need to make your writing process less stressful, more strategic and ideally more lucrative and prolific.

WE SINCERELY HOPE this guide has helped you to understand the workbook in more detail and good luck with the writing. Don't forget to let us know at hackneyandjones.com when your book is finished. We'd love to see how you got on.

HAPPY WRITING!

Advice On Writing By Fellow
Authors

Angela Marsons - Crime Fiction

We asked Angela about her writing process and this is what she told us:

"My tips on generating plot twists is to keep it as natural as possible. They don't have to be big twists as long as you continue to surprise the reader by changing direction here and there. I never start a novel with plot twists in my head, they often come as I'm writing because that's when I'm getting to know the storyline and characters better myself. I think planning is an individual thing. I plan very little and prefer to just get stuck into the writing once I've researched my chosen subject. Normally but the time I've written about ten chapters I have to scribble a timeline on an A4 piece of paper which I add to as I write but if I plan too much it takes both the fun and the surprise out of the writing process for me so I prefer the story to grow organically as I go."

Emma Robinson - Writer of Women's Emotional Fiction

"I write a full synopsis before I begin and I usually use a five-act structure. For my current book, I planned using the 15 beats described in **'Save The Cat Writes a Novel'** by Jessica Brody. I really liked that so will add that to my process. 2. All of my books feature a mother as a central character so I read news stories, blogs and websites aimed at mothers to spark ideas. I also shamelessly pillage the lives of people I know! 3. I use the internet for research but the best research, by far, is talking to people who have been through the same experience as your character. For example, lots of reviews for my book **'My Silent Daughter'** comment on how well researched it is. Apart from a visit to a special needs school, most of that research came from speaking at length to two separate friends who have a child with autism. 4. By putting myself in their shoes and trying to feel what they might feel. Writing character is a lot like acting in that way, I think. Sometimes I have a picture of a person in my head, but not always - I'm not really a visual person. 5. Just write. Even when you don't feel like doing it. Even when what you write is rubbish. Don't edit as you go along. Keep going until that story is down; you can improve it later.

My favourite two inspirational quotes (which I have stuck up on the wall of my writing room):

- 'The worst enemy to creativity is self-doubt' Sylvia Plath
- 'The first draft of anything is shit.' Ernest Hemingway"

Donna Ashcroft - Feel Good Cosy Women's Fiction

1. Do you plan your books, if so how?
I'm somewhere in the middle of a plotter and a pantser. My books are character driven, so I need to know my characters really well before I write anything because that influences their behaviour. Who they are, what they do, what their wounds are, what they need to overcome and what needs to happen in the book to set them on their journey and create their turning points.

This forms the bones of my plot. I'll usually know the first few scenes, turning points, the black moment and final scene. The rest is often organic. I find my best ideas come as I write. I don't like to be tied down to a rigid plot.

2. Where do you get your ideas from?

Life. Movies, books, newspaper articles about events or people. If I get stuck I go for a walk. Being alone in nature helps me to think. I daydream a lot.

3. How/where do you do research?

Google! Before I begin a new book (especially if it's the first in a series set in a new location) then I create the world first. I draw a map (I have colouring pens and A3 paper). I find my characters and save pictures of them in a file, name them, detail their physical characteristics (this is helpful when I want to remember what colour their eyes are when I'm writing). Every book I have written has its own folder. I'm a visual person and it helps me to see things. For **'The Village of New Starts'**, I collected pictures of Scotland – mountains, beaches, lochs, castles, a post office, Scottish high street, a yurt, plus an African parrot and a goat.

If I can, I will visit the area. My locations are made up, but they are based around real places. My last book is set in the Scottish Highlands. I visited the Isle of Arran when I was writing it. I walked up a mountain, saw a lochan, went to the beach, took a distillery tour. It's not essential, but I find it helps to breathe life into the book especially the descriptions.

4. How do you make your characters believable?

I give them flaws - we all have them. I have to know what they want in life and what they need in order to be happy. What their wound is. I try to know them well – what their favourite music is, what they drink, so I can pick these things out to help set them apart. I find the characters come to life as I write, so it's often once the book is finished that I really know them and then I can flesh them out more at the end.

5. Tips for motivation, fear, low confidence..?

Just keep writing. I know it sounds obvious, but it is the only way through. Read Stephen King's **'On Writing'**. Don't give up. Write every day and set yourself realistic goals – even a 50 words a day is better than none. Remember most authors struggle with confidence and fear, it's part of the creative process. You need to be brave enough to work through it. Every book I write I think is terrible. They all make me anxious, especially when I am approaching the middle and end, or when I read through my first draft. Never underestimate the power of a good edit, or editor. A blank page cannot be fixed so fill it with something (I'm not the first to say that, but it's true!).

Peter James - Crime Fiction

When we asked him where he gets his inspiration from, he told us he gets his ideas from local news.

Cara Hunter - Psychological Thrillers

1. Do you plan your books, if so how?
I spend a huge amount of time planning. I'm a *serious* plotster! Most of my books start as a half-page synopsis and grow gradually until they're about 30 pages long. I then start filling that time-line out, layer by layer, adding scenes, dialogue, and eventually I find I have a draft on my hands.

2. Where do you get your ideas from?
All over - from true crime TV or podcasts, from things I see in the newspaper, from interesting faces I see on the street, even from dreams.

3. How/where do you do research?
A lot of it is online, but I do also have a 'pro team' of advisers, who

help with the technical side - police procedure, forensics, legal and medical and so on.

4. How do you make your characters believable?
A lot of it is in the dialogue - I work really hard to make my characters talk like real people. The rhythm of natural speech is so crucial.

5. Tips for motivation, fear, low confidence...?
Keep on keeping on! You'll have blockages, you'll hit obstacles, you just have to 'write your way out of them'. As for confidence - nothing builds that like sheer practice. The more you write the better you will be.

Books We Recommend

Writing guides

Save The Cat - Writes A Novel

Also Published by Hackney and Jones

How to Write a Novel from Scratch

How to Write a Novel from Scratch is created BY authors FOR authors. It guides you from day one, helping you to come up with an exciting book idea from the very start. How to Write a Novel from Scratch covers the WHOLE process of writing a book through clear, logical steps. Simply fill in the blanks. AVAILABLE NOW

Feedback

Thank you for reading 'The Ultimate Guide To Novel Writing For Beginners'. We hope you enjoyed the book? Please now scan the QR code below to leave your feedback.

Feedback

Thank you for reading The Ultimate Guide To Novel Writing For Beginners. We hope you enjoyed the book. Please show us the QR code below to leave your feedback.

www.ingramcontent.com/pod-product-compliance
Lightning Source LLC
Chambersburg PA
CBHW031545080526
44588CB00018B/2702

9 781915 216182